~~~~~~~~

ALL I NEED TO KNOW
ABOUT MINISTRY
I LEARNED FROM
FLY FISHING

~~~~~~~~

~~~~~~~~~

ALL I NEED TO KNOW
ABOUT MINISTRY
I LEARNED FROM
FLY FISHING

~~~~~~~~~

Myrlene L. J. Hamilton

Judson Press
Valley Forge

All I Need to Know about Ministry I Learned from Fly Fishing

Bible quotations in this volume are from the New Revised Standard Version of the Bible, copyright © 1989 by the Division of Christian Education of the National Council of Churches of Christ in the United States of America. Used by permission. All rights reserved.

Interior illustrations by Pani Miller

Library of Congress Cataloging-in-Publication Data

Hamilton, Myrlene L. J., 1952–
    All I need to know about ministry I learned from fly fishing / Myrlene L.J. Hamilton.
        p. cm.
    Includes bibliographical references.
    ISBN 0-8170-1396-2 (pbk. : alk. paper)
        1. Pastoral theology. 2. Fly fishing—Religious aspects—Christianity. I. Title.

BV4011.3.H35 2001
253—dc21
                                                                        2001029292

Printed in the U.S.A.

07 06 05 04 03 02 01

10 9 8 7 6 5 4 3 2 1

In memory of my father
Sidney Jacobson
Who taught me to fish
with worms and a bobber

In honor of my husband
Ed
Who taught me to fish
with flies

With gratitude to God
Who is still teaching me to catch fish
for the Kingdom

CONTENTS

CONTENTS

ACKNOWLEDGMENTS

I WANT TO EXPRESS MY GRATITUDE to the good folks at Judson Press for once again taking a leap of faith with me, with special thanks to Randy Frame for his encouragement during the writing of this book. I also want to thank several people who read part or all of the manuscript in its various stages and provided helpful comments and critique: Rev. David Bowman, Rev. Connie Dorn, Rob Johnson, Laurie Kelly, Larry Merboth, Laurel Olson, Janet Peterson, Lynn Price, Bobby Price, and Terry Walsh.

Thanks, too, to the folks at the West Branch Angler in Deposit, New York, for providing a wonderful place of retreat where weary anglers such as I can find renewal, do a little writing, and (hopefully) catch a few fish.

I am particularly grateful for the constant encouragement from my best fishing buddy (my husband, Ed) and the people of Morning Star Presbyterian Church.

PREFACE

MY HUSBAND AND I were taking a week of combined study leave and fly fishing in the Catskills, near Deposit, New York, where the Delaware River narrows to a trout stream. It was the first time we had tried to combine fishing with working, and I found that my mind began to turn off as soon as we unloaded the Labradors from the back of the truck.

Sleep came easily that week; thinking did not. I did a little writing, some reading, and quite a bit of fishing and dog-walking. Toward the end of the week, my production-driven mind began to emerge from vacation hibernation to analyze what I had accomplished. The answer: very little. I began to feel guilty, even though I knew that our congregation was very supportive of our chosen activity. We needed the break. Still, it was a study leave. So, I began to ask myself a different question: What had I learned? Patience, faith, persistence, humility (all related to my attempts at fishing, not to my reading or writing). It occurred to me that if I were from a different tradition (say, monastic, as opposed to Presbyterian), those learnings might be sufficient. And, even as a Presbyterian, I might find them more valuable than the facts and figures and methods that books could teach me. So, I sat down and outlined what I have learned about ministry from two decades of fly fishing.

According to the *Shorter Catechism*, the chief end of humankind is to glorify God and enjoy God forever. It's easy for many of us to ignore the "enjoy" part and to think that our relationship with God is all work. But I don't believe that God meant for us to box our life into little compartments—now I'm praying, now I'm having fun, now I'm doing ministry. God is involved in all of life, and our lives will be more whole (and our ministry more productive) if we let God teach us through play and love and nature as well as through books and classes and meetings.

This is not a how-to book. I will not try to tell you how to preach or teach or do pastoral care. My hope is that this book will be an inspiration to your life and ministry and that it will motivate you to do more fishing—at the river and in your ministry.

1 :: THE CHIEF END ⊙F FISHING

"Do not be afraid;
from now on
you will be catching people."
—Luke 5:10

I HAVE READ THAT one sign of insanity is when you do the same thing over and over again while expecting different results. I don't know about you, but to me that sounds like the perfect description of fishing.

On an evening in late May, my husband, Ed, and I were fly fishing on the West Branch of the Delaware River in New York. Along with several other diehards, we were flailing the water repeatedly, with no results. We kept doing it anyway. Late in the evening, an older gentleman came along with his fly rod and just sat down on the bank, watching the river. I wondered why he wasn't flailing the water along with the rest of us. Bored with my own lack of action, I went over to speak to him. He told me about the big one he had caught the night before, right in that same spot. Then he pointed to the river. He said, "See that big rock out there? There's a big trout lying right beside it. And there's another one over there and another one over there. When it's just about dark, I'll have about a ten-minute window when they start to rise."

Meekly I asked him, "And when they start to rise, what will they be taking?"

"Rusty spinners," he said.

I went back to my fishing, but kept the old man within eyesight. For luck, I tied on a rusty spinner and resumed my flailing. A few minutes later, I saw a splash in the vicinity of one of his big fish. He was talking with someone else at that moment, so I kindly pointed out to him that maybe it was time to start fishing.

He took his rod, stepped out in the river, and cast a couple of times. Then he came back in and said, "No point killing myself before it's time." And he sat back down. I went upriver, still keeping him in view. The sun went down, and the sky darkened. Finally, the old man unfolded himself, stretched, and stepped into the river. He made one cast, and a fish rose, grabbed that rusty spinner, and snapped off the leader. I don't know what the old man did then, because I, along with the other flailers, reeled in and went back to the cabin.

In fly fishing, you have to learn the ways of the river and the ways the fish interact with their environment.

In fishing, it seems that there is always someone who knows the magic—the magic spot, the magic fly, the magic time of day. And it's always someone else.

In ministry, there are often similar frustrations. We keep doing what we do (sometimes ad nauseum) with marginal success, while our colleague down the street, or in the next town, reels in the big ones with seemingly little or no effort. Our neighbor's creel is full, while ours remains pitifully empty.

But magic has little if anything to do with catching fish, or with being successful in ministry. In fly fishing, you have to learn the ways of the river and the ways the fish interact with their environment, especially the insects. You need to spend time, not just in books, but out on the river, watching, learning, failing. In time, what seems like magic becomes almost second nature. In ministry, too, it's not just book learning but education on the river that yields maturity and success. One whose calling is to fish for people must find the answers to some pertinent questions. What are people hungry for? What are their great desires? Where do they spend their time? How do they respond to various kinds of "bait"?

More than that, the one who is called to fish for people must spend
time out on the river with the One who created the fish and the bugs
and the river itself.

:: FISHING OR NOT ::

Let's begin at the beginning. If the fisher of persons wants to find success in ministry, the first question to ask is, "Am I fishing or not?"
Because we are preaching every week, visiting people in the hospital,
and teaching Bible studies, we tend to think we are fishing. But we
may just be dangling our toes in the water and getting a tan. Ed and
I choose our fishing spots not just for the quality of the fishing but
also for the quality of the environment. If we find a place we like, we
tend to go back again and again. It becomes like a mini-home away
from home where we go to get away from it all. On the first evening,
we unpack and unwind. We may not get our fishing gear out until the
next day. Sometimes we will go through a whole week without fishing very hard. We just like being there—being quiet, watching the
river go by, letting down. And that's okay, until someone asks us how
the fishing is going. "Oh, it's a little slow," we might say vaguely.
Truth is, it's not going at all. We're just coasting. Oh, we'll get around
to fishing, once we're done with our loafing.

That's okay for vacationers, but such coasting should not be confused with fishing.

What's true for many ministers (both clergy and laity) is that
we're vacationing instead of fishing. We are very busy doing many
things, and we are enjoying each other, enjoying the river going by.
At the same time, our community is growing, the population bur-
geoning. The schools are overcrowded. "Why aren't some of those
people coming to our church?" we ask. Well, it just could be that we
aren't fishing. We're just sitting on the porch, sipping sarsaparilla
with our friends, having a great time.

4   When Jesus said to Peter, "From now on you will be catching people," he wasn't joking. That's our job.

I don't say that to spark guilt in those who live in declining communities or rural areas, where there are few unchurched people to reach. Not every church is meant to be a megachurch. But churches are meant to grow, both in spiritual maturity and in numbers. Something should be happening out there.

:: FISHING OR CATCHING ::

There are lots of styles of fishing. You can fish with a bobber and a worm on the end of a long string; you can walk along a stream with a fly rod; you can troll your spinner behind a boat; out in the ocean you can let your line go way down deep with heavy weights and bait; you can use a dip net or a spear. You can fish with worms, or squid, or spinners, or flies.

While there is an endless array of fishing styles, there are only two types of fishing. One is where you go fishing and don't catch anything. The other is fishing and catching.

Fishing and not catching is something I know a lot about. In fact, this kind of fishing is very popular with many people. And it's easy to master. You don't have to bother learning a whole lot about the environment or the equipment or the fish. Just go fishing and see what happens. Good luck.

In some ways, this is the best kind of fishing, because you can have a nice day outdoors, and when you come in, there are no stinking, slimy fish to clean. At the heart, it's a whole lot like not fishing—though you are out there making a good show of it. There are hazards, though. Just when you think you are going to make it through the day and not catch anything, there's a tug on the line. *Then* what do you do? That happened to my niece Laurel when she was about fourteen. She and the rest of her family had come to

visit Ed and me in Alaska. And what do you do in the summer in
Alaska? Well, you go salmon fishing. When we got to the river,
there were no fish in evidence. In fact, we were pretty sure they had
already gone all the way upstream. Still, most of us were concentrating hard on being ready for that strike to happen. Except Laurel.
Laurel seemed bored as she casually made her first cast. All of a sudden, it happened. A fish grabbed her line and took off. She
screamed, and nearly lost the rod. She did lose the fish. No one else
had a hit all day.

A lot of churches are like that. They're out there fishing, all
right, but not much is happening, and when they do get a strike,
they don't know what to do. And more often than not they spook
the fish. A church that we served a few years ago said that they
wanted to get more young families in the church, and that was one
thing that drew us there to serve as their pastors. The problem was
that whenever a young family would come, they would get "the
stare." Sometimes, if they had a restless young child, they would
even get "the boot." "The cry room is upstairs," one couple was told
rather gruffly by an older member of the church. The young couple
never came back.

:: CATCH AND RELEASE ::

For those who are committed to fishing and catching, there is one
more critical decision: catch and kill or catch and release?

Catching and killing is no doubt the more popular of the two,
because most of us want to bring home a trophy—and lots of us like
to eat fish. If we were to translate this into our church work, we may
think that we are gathering up all those fish for our own benefit, our
own use. We want to catch more people because we need more
money in the offering plate, or we need more teachers, or more
whatever. I suspect that we have all seen churches that are really

6

good at the catch-and-kill kind of fishing. They reel everybody in, sit them down, and then squeeze all the enthusiasm and creativity and life out of them—or else bore them to death. Someone once said that the only real heresy is to make the gospel boring. Amen to that! God is anything but boring.

Sometimes when we hear about fishing for people, we are afraid it's the catch-and-kill type. I think this is one reason why evangelism is something that people tend to avoid. It has a predatory feel to it. But this is not the kind of fishing that Jesus invites us to participate in.

The kind of fishing that Jesus wants to teach us is catch and release.

The kind of fishing that Jesus wants to teach us is catch and release. I started to learn about catch and release at about the same time I was learning fly fishing. A favorite fishing stream in Oregon, the Metolius, has beautiful native rainbow trout cohabiting with hatchery-raised planters. If you catch one of the natives, you are required by law to respect that fish's right to life and let it go back into the stream. (Hatchery raised fish have the adipose fin clipped off.) To make it easier on the fish, you have to use flies only and barbless hooks.

When Jesus spoke to Simon about catching people (Luke 5:10), the word translated as "catching" literally means to take them alive. Catch and release. Reel them in for Jesus Christ and the kingdom of God, and then set them loose to become what God has called them to become. In our church's vision statement, we say that we want to help people "meet Jesus Christ and grow spiritually." That's the fishing and catching part. Then we say that we want to "enable each person to discover and enter into the unique ministry God has given him or her." That's the release part. Each person is unique and is valued by God. Each person has a special calling from God. We don't want to force people into molds, because when we do that, we just get (excuse the old joke) moldy Christians.

This kind of fishing is risky business because people may not become what we want them to become, and we may not fill all the "slots" on our nominating slate. These folks may even create new ministries that we had never even dreamed of. God forbid, they may even take what they learn from us and go and join a different church!

Even so, I have come to believe that the chief end of fishing is catch and release. Our "fish" may not turn out the way we thought, but they'll become what God wants them to be, and so will we.

2 :: THE LANGUAGE OF FISHING

*Nevertheless, in church I would
rather speak five words with my mind,
in order to instruct others also,
than ten thousand words in a tongue.*
—1 Corinthians 14:19

LIKE ANY OTHER SPORT, fly fishing has its own vocabulary. If you're going to keep up with the fly-fishing Joneses, you'd better know the difference between a leader and a tippet, a Royal Wulff and an Isonychia. For good measure, throw in some dubbing material and a zinger or two.[1] The people at the fly shop will be impressed. Your non-fly-fishing friends will be in awe.

But the fish won't be. Fish are intelligent, but not all that esoteric. What the fish care about is, "Do you know what I like to eat for supper, and can you serve it the way I like it? If you know what I like to eat for supper, and you come out to my place, well, I might come out to see you."

---

1. *A tippet is a length of fine monofilament. Anglers attach the tippet to the end of a leader and tie the fly onto the tippet. Using tippet material preserves the leader and, in theory at least, saves money. The Royal Wulff and the Isonychia are types of flies. Dubbing material is natural or synthetic fiber used in tying flies. A zinger is a gadget that fly fishers pin on their vests. The retractable cord on the zinger has a snap to which the angler can attach another gadget such as a light, a hemostat, or other necessary fishing gear.*

10   Ministry has its own vocabulary, too. I learned some really neat theological words when I was in seminary—eschatology, theophany, propitiation, to name but a few. In the context of the academic/spiritual community and my spiritual growth at the time, those words touched me, even moved me, because of what I was learning. I was eager to use them on the "fish" when I got out of school. The fish were not impressed. They wanted to know something else. Did I understand what they were going through? Did I know where they were hurting, and did I care?

Very often, church leaders have a language problem with their people. The leaders are talking in ecclesiotheological jargon. Denominational code words, theological buzzwords, archaic hymn words. An example: One of my favorite hymns is "Come, Thou Fount of Every Blessing." It speaks to me; it always has. I love to sing it. But I don't choose it to sing at a Sunday morning service at my church. Why? In a typical worship service, there's no time to translate the hymn for people. "Here I raise my Ebenezer" goes right by most folks, even those who are somewhat biblically literate. The concept of the Ebenezer (which in Hebrew meant "stone of help") is powerful and has great depth of meaning, but we might just as well be speaking in tongues if the congregation doesn't understand what it is.

We need to speak a language that will communicate God's grace to them—the language of love.

In ministry our fish are talking their own language. Words such as marriage, divorce, problems with kids, loneliness, depression, hope, fear, plans, and dreams all have meaning to them. It's not that the people aren't intelligent enough to learn the big words. They just are not in a place where such words are relevant or meaningful. But they do want God to connect with them. They want the reality behind the big words. If we want to "hook" our people, we need to speak a language that will communicate God's grace to them—the language of love.

:: READING THE WATER ::

One of the most valuable skills for the fly fisher is to learn to "read" the water. Trout like to hide behind big rocks and below undercut banks with overhanging tree roots. At the head of a pool, they are likely to position themselves on either side of the current, or under the current, where the water slows a bit, in order to have the best vantage point for watching the bugs that are being swept along. They like deep, clear, weedless pools, where they can easily see their prey, and they often hang out in eddies, where food is plentiful. It helps, too, to know that trout face upstream, with their noses into the current. If you know the direction a fish is facing, then you will know where to place the fly. Otherwise you can cast all day with perfectly good flies and catch nothing.

Like other fish, trout tend to hang out with other trout. Where you find one, you will more than likely find more.

They call it reading the water, but it's really about the behavior patterns of the trout. And you would read things differently if you were after a different species of fish. Bass, for instance, hang out in the weeds. At different stages of life, fish behave differently, too. The small fry will snap at anything that remotely resembles a fly. The older the trout, the cagier and more patient they become.

One of the most embarrassing fishing trips we ever took was to the Russian River in Alaska. We had fished other streams with some success, but the Russian was famous for its millions of sockeyes. If you can catch fish anywhere, it should be the Russian. Why, you could hardly step into the river without stepping on one.

When we got there, it was "combat fishing" at its worst. People were standing shoulder to shoulder on both sides of the river, irritating each other as well as the fish. We pulled out our specially tied (by a friend) Russian River flies and cast out to the middle of the stream—and cast, and cast.

There was very little action that day, but from time to time, someone would hook a fish and cry, "Fish on!" We didn't have a nibble.

What seemed strange, other than the lack of action, was that people seemed to be fishing awfully close to the banks of the river. What we finally learned (too late for that day's fishing) was that unlike some other types of salmon, sockeyes tend to hug the bank. Go figure.

Many churches go fishless, not for lack of activity, but simply because they are fishing where the fish are not.

Churches today would do well to learn to "read the water" in the communities where they live. There are several good ways to do this. There are organizations that can provide helpful demographic studies of your ministry area. Such a study will quickly tell you whether the "fish" you are after are living in your area. If you want to start a ministry to senior citizens, and the demographics indicate a very low population of seniors, you may want to reconsider. Phone or door-to-door surveys can also provide vital information about the local area. Choose your questions carefully, though. There was a church, for instance, that had been started in a large metropolitan/suburban area, where there were already a dozen Presbyterian churches. A survey was done in the ministry area of the new congregation before finalizing plans to start the new church. Results of the survey showed that an abundance of Presbyterians lived in the area. So, the new church was started. The church had a bumpy, slow start, and nearly died. When I started my ministry in that congregation some fifteen years later, someone commented to me about that survey. It was interesting, they said, that no one asked all those Presbyterians whether they would actually *attend* a new church if it were started! Today, even asking the denominational question can be misleading. In general, people are less committed to a denomination than they are to finding a church that will meet their needs.

In our current ministry, the local area is highly Catholic. But many of those Catholics are disillusioned, and a large proportion of those who are active in our Morning Star Presbyterian Church have a Catholic background. People who live at the Jersey shore are into recreation. Small wonder that programs with a nautical theme are popular. One of our members (we call him "Skipper Eric") teaches a class in sailing techniques and safety. He salts his presentation with just enough Bible quotes to pique people's interest.

Yet another aspect to reading the water involves paying attention to the broad cultural changes that are taking place in our society at large. One of the most important is the death of Christendom. When I refer to the death of Christendom, I don't mean the death of Christianity, or the death of the church, though the word "Christendom" is sometimes broadly used to refer to Christianity. Christendom is the idea that the Christian faith and Western culture are part and parcel of the same thing. To be a good citizen equals being a good Christian.

Christendom began in the fourth century when the Roman emperor Constantine legalized Christianity and gave the church favored status (the end of a long period of persecution). With that act he started a movement that lasted about nine centuries. Constantine and those who followed him made every attempt to create a Christian civilization, a Christian culture. During those nine centuries, it was the church that defined life throughout the Western world. George Hunter says, "Sometimes the Church's influence bordered on monopoly. If people were educated, they got it from the Church. Art and music served christian themes. The church even became a prominent land holding institution."[2] At one time, the church owned a large portion of land throughout Europe, including fully one-fourth of the property in Great Britain and one-third of the property in both France and Germany. Christianity was pervasive in Western culture. Christianity and culture were, so to speak, married.

In the fifteenth and sixteenth centuries, the world began to change. One thing that happened, as you probably know, is that the church became more and more corrupt, and was begging for reformation. The reformation that eventually ensued didn't just repair the

---

2. George Hunter, How to Reach Secular People (Nashville: Abingdon Press, 1992), 23.

14   problems in one church; it broke up a monopoly. The other thing that happened was that "armies of various nobles and barons sacked the monasteries and seized church property; they said at the time that the property was being 'secularized,' that is, withdrawn from the control of the Church."[3] For the past five hundred years, this process of secularization—pulling things out from under the influence of the church—has continued. The marriage between culture and faith gradually disintegrated.[4]

Things began to change more rapidly in the last half of the twentieth century. When I was a kid growing up in South Dakota in the 1950s and 1960s, the church was pretty much the only game in town on Sundays. You couldn't shop on Sunday, and you couldn't buy gas. No school would even *think* of scheduling a soccer game or a baseball game on a Sunday. Now, Sunday is becoming more and more just like any other day of the week. In today's world, the church has become just one of many options that people consider—and for many, not a very important option at that. So, soccer games and little league and the company picnic often provide a more interesting, more important agenda, than attending church.

One Christian author says that the turning point for him was on a Sunday evening sometime in 1963. He writes, "Then, in Greenville, South Carolina, in defiance of the state's time-honored blue laws, the Fox Theater opened on Sunday. Seven of us—regular attenders of the Methodist Youth Fellowship at Buncombe Street Church—made a pact to enter the front door of the church, be seen, then quietly slip out the back door and join John Wayne at the Fox."[5]

The end of the blue laws opened the dam, and the floodwaters

---

3. George Hunter, How to Reach Secular People (Nashville: Abingdon Press, 1992), 25.

4. See Hunter, How to Reach Secular People, 21–39, for a brief but thorough description of the cultural changes that have contributed to secularization from the fifteenth century to the present.

5. Stanley Hauerwas and William Willimon, Resident Aliens: Life in the Christian Colony (Nashville: Abingdon Press, 1989), 15.

have changed the landscape of our world. And by making these significant changes, our culture is now pounding the last few nails in the coffin of Christendom.

As a result, kids growing up today do not hear the Christian message in the public schools. They don't necessarily hear it in the music they listen to or see it in the movies they watch. The culture is no longer immersed in the gospel and its symbols.

Just a few years ago, a London marketing firm asked seven thousand people in Australia, Germany, India, Japan, Great Britain, and the United States to identify nine well-known symbols—among them were the cross, the Olympic rings, and the logos of Shell Oil and McDonald's. Guess which one was recognized by the most people? Ninety-two percent of those surveyed recognized the Olympic rings. The company logos of Shell and McDonald's were recognized by 88 percent. The cross was recognized by 54 percent.[6]

One of the results of the death of Christendom is that a large segment of our population is "ignostic." George Hunter distinguishes ignostics from both atheists and agnostics. Atheists are people who say they don't believe in God. Agnostics are people who say they are not sure what they believe. But ignostics are people who have no idea what we are talking about because they themselves have no Christian memory.[7]

Ed and I began to notice this a few years ago, when young couples would come to us from outside the church to get married. We would talk about Scripture and the Lord's Prayer, and sometimes we would get a blank stare. People sometimes would ask us to baptize a child, more or less as a family ritual, and they didn't have a clue that there was more to it than that. After explaining to a young mother the vows she and her husband would make, and the expectations that we would have about their involvement in the church, she said, "Whoa! That's a whole 'nother commitment!" I said, "Yeah, it is."

6. "Burgers Best the Cross," Youthworker Update, November 1995, 3.

7. Hunter, How to Reach Secular People, 41.

16 She left my office thoughtfully, and didn't return.

Christendom is fading fast. Will it surprise you to hear me say that I am not all that sorry to see it go? Here's the reason. The upside of Christendom is that the gospel is well known. It's expected that the population will be "Christian" in attitude and behavior. But the downside is that the meaning of Christian commitment gets watered down. Many people in a "Christian" society are nominal Christians at best. Besides that, in Christendom, the church becomes lazy; we expect the culture to spread the gospel for us. Now that Christendom is gone and the story is not known, it becomes more and more clear that the message will not be spread unless we do it. In other words, in our post-Christendom world, the Church gets both its job and its identity back.

:: MATCHING THE HATCH ::

On sunny midsummer afternoons on the Metolius River in central Oregon, a wonderful insect called the green drake emerges. The local trout are wild about them. When we were fortunate enough to be fishing in the middle of a green drake hatch, I would sometimes stop fishing for a while and just watch the choreography of the fish rolling, snatching, leaping for those fat, juicy insects. The local fly shop did a booming business with their green drake imitations, and we bought our share. They were big flies, in a two-tone green, with a thick hackle.[8] I liked them because they were easy to see on the water.

It was the green drake that taught me what it means to "match the hatch." When the drakes are hot, that's all the fish can think about. So, if you want action while the drakes are hatching, tie one on.

When we moved east, I had some western green drakes in my fly box, and I was eager to use them. I discovered quickly, and much to

---

8. *Hackle is a kind of tying material, typically made of feathers.*

my disappointment, that eastern flies are not the same as western flies. That's because eastern bugs are not the same as western bugs. They are daintier, smaller. And the imitations are, of necessity, less heavily adorned. I had to retire (at least temporarily) the overdressed western green drakes and get acquainted with some new favorites, like the Isonychia.

It may seem complicated at first, but matching the hatch is simply a matter of sharpening one's skills of observation while learning some basic principles. What flies are likely to be hatching at any given time of year or day? Of those, which flies are actually hatching, and of those, which ones are the fish feeding on? Several hatches may be going on simultaneously. Just because a particular bug is hatching doesn't mean that it's the preferred fare for the trout.

When studying the entomology of the stream, one quickly becomes acquainted with nymphs, emergers, duns, and spinners. The different life cycles of the caddisfly, mayfly, and stonefly become apparent. The question to ask is, What are the fish hungering for?

The question to ask is, What are the fish hungering for?

Matching the hatch when fishing for people is not much different. It essentially means sharpening your skills of observation and caring more about what they really need than what you want to feed them. What they really need, of course, is to know Jesus Christ and to follow him. But that need is often hidden under layers of other *felt* needs—loss, addiction, economic setbacks, relationship problems, marriage and family issues, and the like. What are people turning to in order to try to fill that emptiness inside? If we want to catch the people in our community, we need to be addressing some of these issues. In other words, the church needs to be perceived as relevant in people's real lives. God certainly is.

A great biblical example of matching the hatch is Paul's sermon in Athens (Acts 17:16–34). Paul had noticed that among all the various idols, there was a statue to an unknown god. He made use of the

18 people's high interest in religion to point them to Christ. "What therefore you worship as unknown, this I proclaim to you" (v. 23). He had their attention because they loved to hear about a novelty.

The fish in our contemporary stream tend to be quite spiritual, but not necessarily "churchy." In addition, many have embraced a philosophy that is coming to be known as "postmodernism."

Postmodernism is a product of our media and technology culture. People who are postmodern are heavily influenced by television, computers, MTV, movies, and electronic gizmos of all kinds. For postmoderns, the pursuit of individualism and materialism has isolated people to the extent that they are starved for community.

Many postmodern people belong to the baby buster generation, but not all. Some are baby boomers and older. While they may isolate themselves in front of their computers, they also want to get "out there" into life. These are the people who go out for extreme sports—skydiving, rock climbing during lunch break, survival training on vacation.

Postmoderns look at life from a holistic perspective; they want to see the big picture. But they don't tend to think in a linear fashion (A + B = C). Multitasking is second nature.[9] Postmoderns tend to be comfortable with body piercing and tattooing because these kinds of markings are a way of indicating a spiritual experience. After all, we are living in a brand culture. Brands express meaning and value. Should it surprise us that people want to brand themselves?

Instead of going to WalMart, your postmodern friend is more likely to go on-line to shop at a site such as eBay. Why? Because it's not just shopping, it's an *experience*. Shoppers set the prices, and they become Internet buddies with people who have similar interests. "From 1995 to 1998, eBay did no outside advertising; yet it boasted 3.8 million registered users and grew from 289,000

---

9. *If you are a fly fisher, you already know about multitasking. It takes the skill of a juggler to handle a rod, net, and slippery fish, all the while trying to stay standing upright in a raging current.*

items in 1996 to 2.2 million today. With a $23-billion market, eBay is now worth more than Kmart, Toys R Us, Nordstrom and Saks combined."[10]

Postmoderns crave community. They want to connect. But they will not connect on a superficial, philosophical level. They're going to connect with us where we really live. And if it doesn't ring true, they'll do their church surfing elsewhere.

If we want to attract postmodern, post-Christendom ignostics into our church, we've got to work at matching the hatch. Sounds complicated, doesn't it? It's not, really, but it will take some effort on our part. And it may require that we make some changes. We need to learn their language. We need to get into the digital world. We need to be as high-tech as we can possibly be. We need to be on the Web.

Am I saying that we need to ditch tradition in favor of whatever cultural wave washes over us? By no means. I mean to suggest that we must discern the difference between form and substance in our life of faith. The gospel message is substance. Hymns and praise songs are different forms of worship. Love and compassion and justice are substance. A tall-steeple church and a storefront ministry in a mall are two different expressions of the church community. We must hold fast to the substance of our faith while holding lightly the outward forms and styles.

Leonard Sweet, professor of postmodern Christianity at Drew University Theological School in Madison, New Jersey, suggests four ways that the church can successfully connect with postmodern people. Using the acrostic "EPIC," he says that we need to be experiential, participatory, image-driven, and communal.[11] It seems to me that these things are right up our alley. We have the greatest *experience* to share with the world: knowing the God of the universe through Jesus Christ. Talk about an extreme adventure! Also, we believe in the

10. *Leonard Sweet, "The Quest for Community," Leadership, Fall 1999, 33.*
11. *Ibid.*

priesthood of all believers, and that means that everyone can *participate*. And what great *imagery* we have: the down-to-earth images of the Lord's Supper and baptism. Perhaps we can dare to add some other imagery familiar to our culture—drama, dance, video. And what better place is there in the world to create a healing and welcoming *community* than the church?

:: THE FINE ART OF IRRITATING FISH ::

Whoever invented the saying "Preachers need to comfort the afflicted and afflict the comfortable" must have either had teenagers or had been on a fishing trip in Alaska. You think it's frustrating fishing on a river or lake and no fish shows a fin all day? Try fishing on a small stream in Alaska. The fish are crowded into the stream like taxis crowd the New York City streets during rush hour, but when you throw your best bait at them, they just move aside. Total disinterest. Kind of like teenagers when you ask them, "How did you like the sermon today?" Yawn.

When we first went fishing for salmon in Alaska, we had to experience quite a paradigm shift. We were used to baiting hungry fish. But *these* fish were on a mission. They had one thing on their minds as they swam upriver: spawn. Food was the farthest thing from their mind. Some more experienced Alaska anglers taught us that spawning fish do not take the bait because they want to eat it. They attack the bait because it irritates them. In fact, if you want to catch a salmon swimming upriver, you have to get its attention. Irritate the fish a little, so it will snap at your spinner or fly or salmon egg bait.

Ministry sometimes reminds me of fishing in Alaska. Many people today are living with the illusion of contentment. And they are on a mission. They are superbusy, active in their community, working hard to make a living and raise their kids right. In fact, they are doing everything *except* making a vital connection with God. They are supercharged with their own agenda, their mission in life. If you toss out a message of hope and healing, the grace of God, more than likely they will just move aside. No time for that now, I've got things to do.

If we are serious about fishing today, we need to learn the fine art of irritating the fish so that they will grab at the grace of God that we are extending. Now, I know what you're thinking. Most preachers are already irritating enough. (So are a whole lot of other church folks.) I'm not giving permission to let all those negative personality traits take over. What I mean is, we need to expose the truth that many people are not as happy as they pretend to be, that there is an emptiness they are trying to fill with all that activity and accumulation, and that God has what they truly need and what, in their heart of hearts, they really want.

:: TRUST THE LOCALS ::

His name was A. B. King, and I will never forget him. He was in his seventies when we met him, and he had fished in central Oregon all his life. He was a master of the Metolius, a river that Ed had loved since he was a boy. And fortunately for us, he was a member of Community Presbyterian Church in Redmond, where Ed and I were serving as interim pastors.

I fell in love with the Metolius the first time that Ed took me fishing there. Spring-fed at its headwaters and at several places along the way, the Metolius is a beautiful example of rushing, pure, clear water. Trout heaven. And the river was good at keeping secrets.

Like all anglers, A. B. loved regaling his audience with tales of his conquests. I would see him at choir practice on Wednesday nights, and he would chuckle, telling me how many fish he had caught that day. I was more than a little jealous. But then came the day that A. B. said, "How would you and Ed like to come along with me, to my secret spot?"

"Oh, yes!" There was no hesitation.

We agreed to go the next Monday, our day off. He encouraged us to sleep in. "No point getting to the river before noon," he said. "We're going down into the canyon. The sun doesn't even hit the river before then." Now that was our kind of day-off fishing! He also warned us that if there was any wind, the trip would be off, because any wind would be multiplied by the canyon walls, and the flies wouldn't stay on the river. To our great delight, all conditions were "go" for the appointed trip. We drove together about twenty miles, driving beyond the sage and juniper into the tall pines of the Cascades, into the area we knew was Metolius country. A. B. did not drive into any of the campgrounds where we knew there to be access points to the river. Instead, he took us on a gravel road that appeared to go away from the river. He turned off onto a dirt path and parked beside a tall pine. "Now we walk," he said. The river was nowhere to be seen. But walk we did, down a path that led to the edge of a canyon wall, and far down below, the rushing river. It was a beautiful sight, but still far away. We had been to this part of the river, but on the other side, which was accessible by car. "Better holes on this side of the river," A. B. said, and started walking down the canyon. Now, remember, this was a seventy-year-old man. He danced down the side of the canyon like a thirty-year-old. We followed a little more slowly, and very cautiously, along the old deer trail that zigged and zagged its way to the bottom of the canyon. When we finally got there, A. B. was patiently waiting, pointing to the first hole.

A. B. didn't bother with a vest and all the fancy accouterments that most fly fishers spend hundreds of dollars on. He just had a few homemade flies stuck in his ragged old hat and a rod that was a trusted friend. "I usually catch one right here," he said. He tossed his fly onto the water, and a feisty trout snatched it right up. After he had expertly landed the fish and returned it to the water, we consulted with him about his fly. "Most people are all hot about green drakes," he said. Well, we knew about the green drakes. The guy at the fly shop had sold us a bunch. "I just tie up these little white things," he continued. His "little white thing" caught several more as we walked down the river and back. What was even better was that both Ed and I caught some too, in some of the most beautiful holes in the river we had ever seen.

That one afternoon at the Metolius changed our fishing life. For one thing, we got hooked on that canyon. We already loved the river, but now it was a passion. My best fishing memories are from that river. All because an old fisherman shared his secret.

The locals you gain the most from in a ministry situation may not be pastors. Like their counterparts on the river, these anglers may hold tight to their secret holes and favorite flies. One who is willing to share is worth his or her weight in gold, but they are truly a rare breed. In our current ministry, most of the locals who have given us pertinent information about the river have themselves been fish waiting to be caught. While we were in the process of looking for a house, we discovered that the real estate agent was a Christian without a church home. Ed asked her what it would take for her and other busy people like her to come back to church. She said, "A nine o'clock service." Her answer was right on the mark. People in this area are busy to the max. Those who have not already made a commitment to be in worship have filled up their Sunday with other things. Casting our nets at the traditional eleven o'clock hour would not catch them; but an early service had a chance. People could come to worship and still have most of the day ahead of them. That's especially true in the summer here on the Jersey shore, where people want to hit the beach well before noon. I know that this sort of thing grates on the nerves of committed church people. "Folks ought to put church first," we say. But remember, we are talking about people who are not yet committed. How are we going

We already loved the river, but now it was a passion.

to catch them if we don't make our services accessible? Don't forget that the eleven o'clock hour originated with the needs of the farmers, who needed time to get their chores done before driving several miles into town to attend worship. We started our church with one service at nine o'clock. More recently we have added a Saturday evening service and a Sunday service at eleven o'clock to see what other fish are out there. But our nine o'clock service remains the most popular by far.

Another valuable source of information for our ministry here has been the former members of a new church start that was aborted. They shared with us what about the ministry had worked and what didn't work, and warned us of some of the hazards in the water.

In every congregation, every ministry situation, every community, there are secrets to be learned.

Whenever we hatch what sounds like a great scheme, we check with our local fishing authorities for their input. Not long ago, I became very intrigued with a fundraising idea that had netted a tidy sum for a church in a town near Philadelphia. It was an auction of fine art, an event that sounded like fun but also potentially lucrative. The group that sponsored the fundraiser was very professional and had a great reputation. We would not be asked to make any monetary investment in the event. We had nothing to lose, it seemed to me. Auctions of fine art are black-tie affairs, but people in our town prefer the T-shirt, blue jeans, and sandals look. Our locals suggested that for our community, a flea market would go over much better, where people could wear their casual clothes and find a bargain. They were right, as usual. I scrapped the idea of the art auction, and a few months later we had a very successful flea market.

Local wisdom should not be confused with the rigid perspective often expressed as "We've never done that before" or "It's never worked here." There's a not-so-subtle attitude difference between the two. Local wisdom is not afraid of risk. It just has an uncanny ability to discern when risk is more likely to pay off. Local wisdom wants God's kingdom to succeed and ministries to thrive. Those who hold the rigid "We've never done that before" attitude won't risk—ever—and control is the goal, no matter what the price.

In every congregation, every ministry situation, every community, there are secrets to be learned. We, as ministers, come in fresh with great ideas that the people at the theological fly shop have sold us. They may truly be great ideas, and theologically sound. But they will not compete with the information the locals can give us about the river itself.

♂ :: BASICS

*If I proclaim the gospel, this gives me
no ground for boasting, for an obligation
is laid on me, and woe to me if I do not
proclaim the gospel! For if I do this of my
own will, I have a reward; but if not of my
own will, I am entrusted with a commission.*
—1 Corinthians 9:16–17

:: WHEN THE FISH CATCHES YOU ::

WHEN YOU CATCH A FISH, it's great sport. When the fish catches you, you'd better hang on, because you're in for the ride of your life.

I wish I could have been standing on the beach at that moment when the "large fish" of the Old Testament vomited Jonah out onto the dry land. Poor Jonah, wet, disheveled, disoriented, scraping kelp out of his hair, gasping for his first breath of fresh air in three days. Poor Jonah, struggling to stand upright, and when he does, the first thing he hears is a familiar voice: "*Now* will you go to Nineveh?"

Jonah slumps back down on the ground and rolls his eyes. "Oh well, sure, now that I know you're serious. Yeah, let me at those rotten Ninevites." Less than enthusiastic, he pulls himself together and preaches hellfire and damnation until the Ninevites are on their knees

28   begging for mercy. Then, he greets their repentance with disdain and shakes his fist at God for making him watch his enemies get right with God. The closing words of the story show a grumpy old prophet feeling sorry for himself and getting a lecture from God about grace.

It's just about the best fish story ever told. And what's so great about it is that it's not about catching the fish. It's about the fish catching the prophet.

And that's a story we all know something about. We all have our own story about God's call on our life. And we have all seen our share of "Ninevites." You know who they are. It's the nasty neighbor who dumps kitty litter on the church lawn. It's the recalcitrant elder who badgers you at every board meeting. It's the town you never wanted to move to, but somehow, God put you there. Maybe it's the ministry itself, a mangy mixture of people's problems, potlucks, and small miracles—a place you never thought you'd be.

I still remember the first time I felt God's tug on the other end of the line.

I still remember the first time I felt God's tug on the other end of the line. I was six years old or thereabouts and was with my family at a Sunday evening church service. Such services were rare at my country church, especially evangelistic ones, which this one was. I remember standing eyeball to eyeball with the backside of the pew near the rear of the small sanctuary. The evangelist was just ending his sermon and was giving an invitation to come forward and accept Jesus as Lord and Savior. Well, that was the first time I had heard about that, but there was something in what he said that connected with my young soul. God was talking to me. I needed to do it. Of course I couldn't, though. I was too little. Too shy. What would my family say if I made that kind of a scene? To my great relief, though, the evangelist relented. When no one came forward, he said we could receive Jesus right where we were. For a shy little girl in a very private family, that was the best news since indoor plumbing (which our little church did not have).

I don't know what I expected to happen after that. But what did happen was that God never stopped tugging. The tugging just got stronger as I grew older. It was when I was in high school that the strange thought began to emerge that God was calling me into the ministry. *The* ministry. As in, going to seminary and then preaching for a living. I even pictured myself in a black robe, even though the pastors in my church didn't wear robes.

Unlike Jonah, I wanted desperately to say yes. But like Jonah, I went the other way instead. I wanted to say yes, but I just couldn't. When I would make a list of pros and cons, the cons won every time. There was no precedent in my family, and while my family was Christian, we tended to take everything in moderation (this would *not* be considered a moderate move, I was sure). In my immediate family, everyone was a farmer, a teacher, a housewife, or a nurse. This was the late 1960s, and while the feminist revolution had begun, it had not made great strides in rural South Dakota. I was shocked when I went to Bible camp as a sophomore and my counselor was a young woman seminarian. Why, I never!

The tugging continued, and every time I felt the tug, I would consider the proposition. Weigh the pros and cons, feel the desire. Talk to one or two people I trusted. One of the first people I talked to was my pastor. He was a little too enthusiastic about the idea in my opinion. That cooled me off a little. Then he gave me a little book of ministers' personal testimonies to read. Though I couldn't relate to the specific details of any of the stories about any of these men, I could relate to the feeling, that sense of call that is indescribable but so real. Each of the vignettes ended with Paul's "Woe to me if I do not proclaim the gospel." I didn't feel particularly woeful, but I knew this was about me. My heart burned within me, but I just couldn't. Not only did I have that list of great excuses, but I also had no money. What would I eat? Manna?

Partway through college, the tugging got to me again, and I talked with a couple more people. One of them was a leader in my college Christian fellowship. He suggested that I consider Christian education, since I was, after all, a woman. I have great respect for those who are called to a ministry of Christian education, but I knew that was not for me. I have teaching gifts, but my call was to *the* ministry. The conversation was discouraging, enough to help me ignore the tugging for another year or so. Then the fish got me. The first big bite came when I was on the verge of being engaged. My would-be fiancé and I were talking one day, and I thought I better tell him this harebrained scheme of mine. So I did. You want to know what he said to me? "You can preach to our kids." That did it. My reaction was not instantaneous, but it was definitive. I realized that I wasn't being true to myself by getting engaged to him. So I dumped him, not very kindly, I'm afraid.

The fish was gaining on me. The associate pastor at my college church, along with his wife, swallowed me up into their family along with some of my friends and just loved me until I finally could give myself permission to say yes. They talked with me and prayed with me and encouraged me. There has never been a time in my life when I felt more a sense of promise combined with fear.

Oh, I was in the belly of the fish by now, all right. And I was singing hymns with Jonah. But reality would hit soon. I had to tell my mother, and I knew that would be tough. My dad had died several years earlier, and I was the last of four kids to finish college and get ready to be self-supporting. Seminary would break that bubble. When I got my mom's initial reaction, I felt like I had been vomited with Jonah onto that salty shore. My destiny was clear, but I knew then that my joy in saying yes would be laced with anguish along the way. Saying yes to God would displease some of the very people whose approval I desperately wanted. But saying no to the call had become impossible.

In the story about Jonah, one thing that impresses me is the number of times that God intervenes. God "hurled" a great wind, "provided" a big fish, "appointed" a plant and a worm. God also appointed Jonah, though the prophet was distinctly less responsive than the other actors in the drama. What the story leaves me with is the intense awareness that like Jonah, and like Paul, I have a commission. And whatever else I may make of my life, I need to give an account to God of how I have responded to that commission. And I need to pay attention to the signposts that God leaves along the way.

As with Jonah, there have been some days in my ministry when I have shaken my fist at God. Sometimes, I have felt the prophet's despair. Many times, I have had to sit through God's lectures as God has reminded me of what it's all about. Then, I recall what it felt like when the fish caught me and there was no denying my destiny. No denying that God still calls and God still empowers. Even me. And then I can face another Nineveh.

:: THE CAST ::

*"We, for our part, will devote ourselves
to prayer and to serving the word." —Acts 6:4*

For the past several years, I've been concentrating my fly-fishing education on entomology—the bugs. When I started fly fishing in the west, it seemed enough to know just a few flies: the elk-hair caddis, the green drake, and the light Cahill served me well on the limited area that I fished. Once in a while I tried a midge or a stonefly. Then, when we moved east, I felt helpless. My flies weren't working. So, I hit the books. I now know the difference between a caddis, a mayfly, a stonefly, and a midge. I know the stages of the mayfly and the importance of the blue-winged olive on the West Branch of the Delaware River. I carry my streamside guide to insects with me on every trip.

In spite of my increased knowledge of the bugs, my catching did not improve a great deal. Not only was my western fly box inadequate for the east, but also my cast (never great by any standards) had gotten rusty. Our favorite holes on the Metolius in Oregon had not required great distance-casting ability for success. The rivers we began to fish in the east stretched my casting ability beyond its limit. I could see that my flies weren't always reaching the fish, and often when they did, the drag on the line spooked the fish.

When we went fishing with a guide last spring, he commented that he enjoys teaching people to cast who have never fished before more than trying to help an "experienced" angler correct bad habits. Since the latter shoe fits, I can understand exactly what he's talking about. I need to work on my cast. I know it. In fact, I've known it for a few seasons now. I remember when Ed first taught me the basics. I went outside and practiced and practiced. From then on, I knew how to do it. So I just went fishing. I do want to improve my technique, because I want to catch more fish (I wouldn't mind looking graceful in the process). But the idea of starting over is painful. Old habits are hard to break. I know it will take discipline to make the changes I need to make. Plus, I do catch *some* fish.

I was frustrated. Then I read this on the sleeve of a fly-casting video: "If you don't know where the fish lie, but can cast to cover the water with finesse, you are likely to catch fish. If you know where they lie but can neither reach them nor present the fly naturally, you are not even in the game."[1]

Now I was beyond frustrated. I was *convicted*. That statement was about me! My lack of success wasn't about the weather or about the bugs or about how I was holding my mouth. I wasn't catching many fish because my cast was lousy. Well, I *do* want to be in the game. So, I started working on my cast in earnest. I'm a visual learner, so the video helped. So did practice. As my fishing has improved, so has my morale.

As I've been working on my cast, I've been asking myself, "What is it in ministry that is so basic that we wouldn't be 'in the game' without it?" There are so many things that we are called to do (or that we

---

1. Joan Wulff, *Dynamics of Fly Casting: From Solid Basics to Advanced Techniques,* dir. Jeff Pill (Camden, Maine: Down East Books, 1997), *videocassette.*

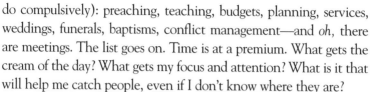
do compulsively): preaching, teaching, budgets, planning, services, weddings, funerals, baptisms, conflict management—and *oh*, there are meetings. The list goes on. Time is at a premium. What gets the cream of the day? What gets my focus and attention? What is it that will help me catch people, even if I don't know where they are?

One would think that after more than twenty years in ministry, I would know what I need to know. If ministry were an assembly line instead of a river with an ever changing environment, that might be true. In my experience, ministry isn't something one learns. It is a series of *learning experiences*. The pastors who do well, whether in large or small churches, are the ones who are willing to keep learning. But that's difficult, especially if it means going back and breaking old, comfortable habits.

I find that I am continually challenged by the spiritual boundaries that the apostles set early in their ministry. Acts 6 tells of an early conflict in which certain Hellenist widows felt neglected in the daily distribution of food. Since the apostles had been in charge of everything in the church up to that time, the concern was brought to them. Now, what would you do? Add another task to your already busy schedule? Squeeze just one more visit into your day? One more meeting? The apostles showed great wisdom when they said, in essence, "Our serving tray is already full. It's an important ministry, but we can't do it personally. You take care of it by choosing responsible people to be the servers. We'll continue doing our job, which is to pray and serve the Word." In the NRSV the quotation is, "We, for our part, will devote ourselves to prayer and to serving the word" (v. 4). If the apostles took on every ministry need that came along, they might neglect their primary ministry. For them, the "cast" was prayer and the service of the Word.

In my experience, ministry isn't something one learns. It is a series of learning experiences.

I believe that's true for us as well. We need to set appropriate boundaries, not just for our own health (that might be reason enough), but also for the sake of our ministry. While we are learning

34 many skills for ministry, we must not neglect the very basic task of prayer and the ministry of the Word. That is where the power is.

I'm not going to tell you how to pray, only that you must do it. Daily, constantly, fervently. With listening ears, and willing feet, as well as a desirous heart. Prayer is the avenue to the heart of God. It is the source of our own strength and direction. It is what changes us, when we open our hearts and lives to God.

I'm not going to tell you how to "serve the Word" either, only that you must do it with all your mind and heart and strength. The basic task of ministers (clergy or laity) is to dispense God's Word. There are many ways to do it. Preachers may do it primarily through their sermons, teachers in their teaching, counselors in their interactions with clients. I'm a great fan of psychological and sociological approaches to understanding and working with people. I've done quite a bit of study in conflict management and the dynamics of church life. We need to keep learning, to keep up with new understandings of our world. But when it comes touching people's hearts, nothing replaces prayer and serving the Word.

To paraphrase Joan Wulff, "If you don't know where the people are but can pray and serve the Word, you are likely to be effective in reaching people. If you know where they are but can neither pray for them nor speak God's word to them, you are not even in the game."

:: FISHER, CATCH THYSELF! ::

*"Doubtless you will quote to me this proverb,
'Fisher, catch thyself!'" —Luke 4:23a, paraphrased*

Fly fishers spend a great deal of time extracting flies from places other than the trout's mouth. Branches, for instance. Or another angler's hat. More than once, I have caught myself. Ouch! Beyond painful, it can also be dangerous, especially if you gouge a hole in your waders.

A similar thing happens when I preach. Very often, the week after I preach, my sermon "catches" me. Double ouch! That's especially painful if it was one of those "relational" sermons— dangerous too, if I let the moment pass without dealing with my own issues.

While catching oneself is a waste of time in fly fishing, it is an essential pursuit when it comes to fishing for people. If you are going to preach to others, or counsel them, or lead them, be sure that you have been caught by your own message. Several passages in the Bible speak to this. The one that carries the most powerful impact for me is 1 Corinthians 9:24–27:

> Do you not know that in a race the runners all compete, but only one receives the prize? Run in such a way that you may win it. Athletes exercise self-control in all things; they do it to receive a perishable wreath, but we an imperishable one. So I do not run aimlessly, nor do I box as though beating the air; but I punish my body and enslave it, so that after proclaiming to others I myself should not be disqualified.

I've been mulling this over while watching the Olympic trials on television and while thinking about the late-summer doldrums that seem to keep summer church attendance down. While preparing a sermon recently, I was tempted: "There won't be that many people there anyway, so. . . ." But Paul says, "Run in such a way that you may win the prize." What an energizing thought! Our ministry is as important (more so) as the events that lead an Olympian to a gold medal. The personal discipline, the focus, the attention, the years of their lives that such athletes give to their sport—most of us church leaders could learn a thing or two. The apostle Paul was one of the greatest fishers of people the world has ever known, yet he did not take his faith or his ministry for granted. Nor did he rest on his laurels. He continued to discipline himself.

I think there's more to it than discipline, though. Mere discipline is a hard taskmaster, and it can lead to a perfectionist lifestyle rather than to mature Christian leadership. Paul's exhortation about running to win comes on the heels of another famous line of his: "I have become all things to all people, that I might by all means save some" (1 Corinthians 9:22). What's tough about both of these challenges is that they are so easy to confuse with codependency (keeping everybody happy, keeping the peace, dealing with other people's issues and not my own) and workaholism (trying to save the world under my own steam, working as an escape from personal problems, filling my life with work instead of dealing with the emptiness in my heart). If we turn Paul's words into codependency and workaholism, we will find ourselves exhausted and ineffective.

Paul's challenge is about focus and purpose. I once heard a sermon titled "Why Do We Do What We Do?" Good question. Why do we do this thing called ministry? Is it for the accolades? For the money? To help people? To feel better about ourselves? Paul says that his discipline is not aimless, nor is it without a purpose. He does it "so that after proclaiming to others I myself should not be disqualified." This suggestion that one might actually preach to others and then be disqualified oneself points to the need for genuineness, authenticity, a real transformed life.

When I said yes to the ministry more than a quarter of a century ago, I knew some things about the task. But I had no clue what it would mean for my character, my personality, my way of life. I began to get inklings when I was in my first call, and I discovered that many of the coping skills that I had grown up with just didn't work any more. I was a shy, scared, little girl in a grownup's skin. I had gifts for ministry and an education to match, but my life skills were sadly lacking. I had to begin to face my lack of assertiveness, lack of boundaries, and difficulty dealing with feelings. I did, but not without struggle. I did it with help of counselors, mentors, and supportive friends. These remain primary issues for me, though I have grown a great deal; I find that when I get lazy in my emotional recovery work, then I snap back to my old ways of relating to life.

And, once again, it doesn't work.

The work of ministry drives me to personal transformation. What I mean by that is that every time I am embroiled in a conflict or controversy or some other kind of hard time, I find that a key to resolution is in facing my own issues. It's easy simply to blame those outside of myself for creating the problem. It's tougher to ask myself, "How must I change in order to work this thing out? Where do I still need to grow?"

I have a dream that recurs from time to time. I've gone back to school, and the sense that I have in the dream is that I'm not sure which end is up. The dream is usually set in my last year or last semester of college. I'm either looking for a place to live or trying to figure out what classes I still need to take in order to graduate. Sometimes, I'm alert enough to have an eerie feeling that I shouldn't have to be there. Didn't I already graduate? Didn't I also go to seminary and go on to get my doctor of ministry degree? Why am I here, back at college, trying to figure out what classes to take and moving into a dorm room? I wake up weary when I have had that dream. It's old news, yet it always points to something new. The dream usually tends to come when I am going through one of those "school of hard knocks" courses. You know, the ones you didn't sign up for but you get to take the exam anyway. The dream reminds me to pay attention to both my heart and my mind as I seek to be open to the changes that God has for me.

A friend of mine likes to tell a joke about an old Pennsylvania Dutchman who used to refer to road signs as "ministers." Someone asked him why, and he said, "Because they point the way, but they don't go there themselves!"

We who talk the talk on Sunday must walk the walk during the week. Well, we know that (didn't I just preach a sermon on that last month?). But what does it really mean for those of us who are leaders in ministry? We need to be leaders in evangelism and stewardship and prayer, certainly. We need to preach our hearts out. We need to work at our ministry and work hard. Beyond that, we need to be able to face our own dark side and deal with our own issues. We need to be leaders in personal transformation. I cannot preach to others unless I am open to God's work in my own life.

:: ESSENTIAL EQUIPMENT ::

"There is need of only one thing. Mary has chosen the better part, which will not be taken away from her." —Luke 10:42

When we head up to the river for our annual fly-fishing vacation, we pack the back of the pickup full of fishing equipment, groceries, clothes, books (well, we *might* have a few rainy days), and Labradors. We like to be prepared. But when it comes right down to it, there are only a few things we need to go fishing: a decent rod and reel, line, a few flies, and waders will get you started. A good streamside guide to flies will fit in your pocket. But most of us have so much fun with the sport that we want more cool stuff. As one nonfishing woman once said, "Give a man a fish, and he will eat for a day. Teach a man to fish and he'll go out and spend thousands of dollars on useless equipment."

Ed and I are both suckers for a good fly shop. Ditto for a good bookstore. Our bookshelves are loaded with commentaries, ministry helps, church-growth books, evangelism books, counseling books— you name it. We have a few videos, too. Good stuff. And it wasn't cheap. It can be easy, though, to get so involved in carrying around all that stuff that we lose track of the few essentials of ministry: the Word of God, the Spirit, prayer, the body of Christ, spiritual gifts, obedience. It's easy to get absorbed (as Martha did) with the outer trappings of our work instead of being immersed in the work itself (as Mary was). Good ministry isn't dependent on having a big church budget so you can buy all the gadgets. It isn't dependent on being busy with lots of projects. It depends on the movement of the Spirit of God among people of integrity and faith. Period.

:: FISHING BUDDIES (PART 1) ::

My beloved speaks and says to me: "Arise, my love, my fair one, and come away." —Song of Solomon 2:10

I'll never forget the first words my husband ever said to me. I was standing in the doorway of my office at the Fircrest Presbyterian Church, near Tacoma, Washington. Ed had just moved to town and was in the process of buying a laundry and dry-cleaning business after an unfulfilling stint as a traveling salesman. He had visited my church a couple of times, but he was an escape artist and had never spoken to me. Then one day, there he was outside my office door, and the first words he said to me were, "I think we have a problem." His mother was getting married and needed a minister, he said. The wedding was going to be on a Monday, which was my day off (hence the problem). I was intrigued by this unusual (and handsome) individual, so I said yes. And our relationship was off and running.

It's interesting how we happen to meet certain people and we become good friends, or we get married. A certain event draws us together and the relationship changes us—changes the direction of our life.

One of the best moments in our relationship came about a year after we were married. Ed asked me if I wanted to go on a fishing vacation. There was no hesitation. "Yes!" I said. Somehow, we had never really talked about fishing before that. When he found out how much I liked it, he said he didn't know that when he married me he got a best friend and a fishing buddy too.

At the time, we didn't know it was going to be *fishing for fish* buddies as well as *fishing for people* buddies. He was still "in the closet" about his call to ministry. But in time our partnership expanded to just about every area of life.

I've been told that there are things that you should never do with your spouse:

40   Never hang wallpaper together (folk wisdom).
Never let your husband teach you to fly fish (fly-fishing expert).
Never serve in ministry together (seminary professor).
We've done them all. And somehow, our marriage has survived. But I can see their point. Hanging wallpaper creates too much intimacy for the power struggle that inevitably ensues. Having your spouse teach you fly fishing gives him or her a potential "one up" position that no marriage needs. (And what if your spouse teaches you incorrectly? Where do you go then?) Then, of course, there's ministry, where a couple serving in an equal position invites all kinds of flack. People try to play you like mom against dad. They compare your sermons (and tell you about it). They complain about one of you to the other. The other problem is that you can never get away from your work. Even in bed. The congregation that I was serving when we got married gave us a signature quilt. We liked it so much that we had it on our bed for years. Ed used to joke that we never could get away from those people.

On the other hand, working and living with someone intimately has its benefits. Our gifts balance each other, and the church gets more for their investment. In the best of worlds, such a marriage and ministry team can be a model for other couples. If we can work our way through those power struggles and strange dynamics that occur in life and ministry, and still find a way to minister to people, then maybe other couples can find a way to work out their relationships too.

We joke about Ed's introductory words to me, "I think we have a problem." But in another sense, that comment defines our relationship. Not that it's problematic, but that we are willing to face problems. Every relationship has its "moments." Every relationship experiences the stress that comes with the growth of one or the other of the partners. Ed and I often talk about the need to renegotiate our relationship. The first time we did that intentionally was when I broke my leg and suddenly had to be chauffeured around instead of driving myself. It may have been the first time, but certainly not the last. With the constant changes that life throws at us these days, it seems like we are renegotiating most of the time. To paraphrase an old saying, "The couple that negotiates together stays together."

:: FISHING BUDDIES (PART 2) ::

Bear one another's burdens, and in this way
you will fulfill the law of Christ. —Galatians 6:2

Ed is my best fishing buddy, whether it's fish or people we are going after. I'm well aware that not every couple in ministry will want to have the kind of close ministry partnership that Ed and I have chosen. And not every church leader is married. But married or not, in ministry with your spouse or not, you need to have some fishing buddies. These are the people you can truly let your hair down with. You can go back to the clubhouse after a grueling day on the river and talk about the successes and the failures—the great catches and the ones that got away. You can put your feet up on the coffee table and speak what's on your mind. There are no pretensions here, no need to make the fish bigger than they really were. These are your friends in ministry, the ones who will stick by you through thick and thin. They may be other pastors or lay leaders in the church. Or maybe they are Christian friends outside your own discipline who share with you a common vision and genuinely care for you as a person as well.

I imagine Jesus and his disciples coming home after a tough day of miracles, sharing laughter and poking fun at each other. Looking to Jesus for that slight nod of the head and the grin that says, "Well done, Peter. Well done, John." In spite of the obvious power struggles that went on between these friends, I sometimes envy the close bond that they had.

Pastors today are notorious for their reluctance to enter into mutually supportive relationships with one another. And I can understand why. Though we are in the same work, we often seem to have little in common—except the feeling of competition. Do I really want to expose my fears and my struggles? To admit that my church isn't doing all that well? Do I want to disclose where all the good fishing holes are? No way.

Most of us have bought into the success model of our culture. If it isn't big and dynamic and powerful, then it isn't worth talking about. And mine needs to be bigger or more impressive than yours. When we have genuine fishing buddies, though, we can find our way back to the true measure of discipleship—faithfulness. Mother Teresa was often quoted as saying, "God didn't call me to be successful, God called me to be faithful." I believe that she hit that nail on the head. Our fishing buddies can keep us honest, and they can challenge us to remember what discipleship is all about.

:: MY KIND OF FISHING ::

"I have said these things to you so that my joy may be in you, and that your joy may be complete." —John 15:11

I've been fishing all my life. I began to choose fishing over other recreation when I was knee-high to a bamboo rod. When my sister Karen and I took two weeks of swimming lessons at a nearby lake one summer, we both learned to dog paddle and do the "dead man's float." I also learned that being in the water didn't intrigue me a bit. I was, however, intrigued by the fact that countless fish swam unseen in those waters. Whenever we went back to that lake, I would make sure I had a fishing pole with me. While the others went in the water, I went in search of the big one.

My weapon in those days was an eight-foot bamboo pole with a long string attached to a hook. A red-and-white bobber completed the ensemble. Earthworms were the bait. On a lucky day, I would also have some big, fat, juicy, white grub worms that my dad and I had dug up by the sheep shed. Those grub worms loved sheep manure. I would sit on the shore of the lake, jam the poor worm on the hook, throw it in the water, and wait. The bobber mesmerized me. I lived for that magic moment that the bobber would begin to ripple the water and then dive. And just at the right moment, I would yank that crappie out of the water and let my dad take it off the hook.

During those same years that I preferred fishing to other pursuits, I was also getting to know God. Somewhere along the line, my parents gave me two gifts that strongly influenced my life. One was a Revised Standard Version of the Bible. The other was a fiberglass Zebco fishing rod with an enclosed reel. My own Bible and my own fishing rod. I attacked both with a passion, reading the Bible through when I was twelve, and repeatedly snarling the line in my enclosed reel. I bugged my dad when he came in from the field on a warm summer night to please, please, please go fishing. He normally acquiesced. And I bugged both my parents to go to any event that had to do with learning about God. In that time and place, the events didn't come along often, but when they did, I wanted to be there. And chances are, if there was an altar call, I would be up front—that, despite my extreme shyness. Something significant was happening in my life, and that something involved fishing and God.

I began to choose fishing over other recreation when I was knee-high to a bamboo rod.

Later in life, I learned that there are lots of ways to go fishing. One could go trolling in a boat, for instance, get closer to where the fish are, and catch perch and walleyes and northerns. One could even go out to the coast, take a seaworthy craft out into the ocean itself, drop a heavy line down to the ocean floor, and catch amazing monsters like halibut.

44   From crappies to halibut, I have loved every kind of fishing I've done. But my life changed when Ed taught me to fish with a fly rod. I still remember when it happened. We had been lake fishing quite unsuccessfully for several days when Ed said, "Let's try some stream fishing." We went to a small stream on Mount Rainier called Skate Creek, Ed with his fly rod, me with my spinning gear (my old Zebco had long since bit the dust). Ed saw a few fish rising in a pool under a bridge, and he gently tossed a fly in their midst. He caught one, and then another. I was captivated by the beauty and the challenge. And right then and there, my fly-fishing education began. After that trip, we went out and bought my first fly rod and reel. Then hip boots and net. Then the vest. Then the fly-tying kit.

Fly fishing appeals to my creative side and to my desire for knowledge. I've had to learn about fish behavior and about the entomology of the river, not just how to cast a fly and land a fish. For me, the greatest success comes when I have analyzed the insect hatches, tied a fly to match, and caught a fish on the fly that I tied. Even getting a rise on a fly that I tied gives me a thrill. I can still enjoy trolling from a boat, and even fishing with a bobber. But my passion is fly fishing.

When I started out in ministry, I expected that I would be a "garden variety" pastor (whatever *that* is). But when I got out of seminary and started work as an interim pastor, I began to learn some things about congregational dynamics, conflict, and seasons in a church's life. Those learnings changed me and how I look at ministry. Although I have spent time as a called pastor in a "regular" church (whatever that is), I have found that I'm most alive in a ministry situation that's a little off the beaten path—interim ministry, for instance, or new-church development. Especially new-church development, because like fly fishing, it appeals to my creative side. I have discovered over the years that I like creating my own curriculum for classes, and I like organizing ministry, writing drama for worship, creating new possibilities. I like learning about the changes in our culture, and trying to figure out what makes people tick. I like the freedom of trying new things. When a new creation succeeds in bringing in more people, I am thrilled.

Well, that's just me. What I am trying to say is that both fly fishing and new-church development have taught me how to be myself. I think that is one of the most important things a minister can learn. It's not an easy lesson, because we have so many preconceptions about what we ought to be like, in life and in ministry. But I believe that God's goal for us is to be fully and joyfully our selves. God created each one of us in the image of God, and as Christians, we are gifted by God with powerful abilities through the Holy Spirit. God wants us to discover who we are created to be and live to the fullest.

Recently, I was talking with a colleague who, along with her husband, was getting ready to go to Cameroon as a missionary. She was commenting on the obstacles our congregation had faced in its start-up. "I just can't imagine being an new-church-development pastor myself," she said.

I laughed. "Well," I said with a grin, "I can't imagine being a missionary in Africa."

:: THE FISH FINDER (PART 1) ::

*"Cast the net to the right side of the boat,
and you will find some [fish]." —John 21:6*

Next to the story of Jonah, the greatest fish story ever told is the one about the great catch of fish pulled in by Jesus' disciples. These professional fishermen have gone fishless all night, when a cocky rabbi tells them where to drop their nets. And then the great haul of fish nearly breaks the nets.

Actually, there are two such stories, one told by Luke early in Jesus' ministry and one told by John some time after the resurrection. This suggests one of two things: either the Gospel writers had a little trouble with their chronology or Jesus kept butting into their business. While the former may be true, the latter is the point I want to make. Jesus is not shy about telling the disciples how to live their lives, even in areas where a carpenter-rabbi would not be expected to have any expertise—like fishing.

I think that there are some areas of life that most of us tend to keep fenced off from God. Suppose you are a neurosurgeon. When you're in the operating room, what do you depend on? Your education? Your memory? Your colleagues? Imagine Jesus coming into the operating room and saying, "Move your scalpel over there just a smidgen and you'll find the problem." Or suppose you are a mechanic puzzling over a knock in the engine. Jesus says, "Hand me that wrench over there, will you?" Then again, suppose you're a pastor working on your sermon. You've just about wrapped up another masterpiece. Jesus says, "I don't think I like your premise." Would you get just a little defensive? Who's the expert here, anyway? Or maybe for you it's the way you manage a checkbook or your time. What would God know about that?

Jesus has no earthly reason to know anything about fishing. Yet, he butts in and tells the fishermen where to cast their nets. I like Simon's response in Luke's version of the story. After explaining that he and the other experts have already come up empty, and there is no use trying, he says, "Yet if you say so, I will let down the nets" (Luke 5:5). *If you say so.* That brief statement speaks volumes. Simon doesn't know Jesus very well at this stage of the game. But he knows enough not to rush to judgment. He is willing try one more time. And he is not disappointed.

The story says a great deal about human nature. We tend to trust our instincts, our training, what we can see and feel and prove. And when we run out of our own resources, we are pretty sure that's the end. But if we are willing to open our minds to what Jesus might do, we will not be disappointed. I've often said that God's best work is done when there is an emptiness, a lack of resources, and human impossibility. It's a common theme in the Bible, this running out of resources (or of not having any to begin with) and having God intervene with miraculous abundance.

So often, we who are leaders in the church, though our intentions are otherwise, grow to trust our human skills and learning. We push God aside while we tinker with the engine. After all, we're the ones getting paid the big bucks. We've had the training. It's our job. We may not even realize that's what we are doing until we run out of steam. What we are doing isn't working, and we're not sure why. And that's when we can take a page out of Simon's fishing journal. Listen to what Jesus has to say. Then, don't rush to judgment. Wait and see what Jesus will do. It's ok to doubt. But then, remember what Simon said: "If you say so."

When we run out of our own resources, then there's room for God to work. Jesus' knowledge is not limited to the vague spiritual realm that we assign to the "religious" among us. He will help us in the day-to-day mundane parts of our life, too.

:: THE FISH FINDER (PART 2) ::

"Yet if you say so, I will let down the nets." —Luke 5:5

Boat fishers in our day outfit their boats with fancy "fish finders" to tell them where the fish are. Fly fishers often hire a guide if they are fishing unfamiliar waters. When it comes to finding fish, though, Jesus is unbeaten. All of the seminars and all of the books and videos about evangelism and church growth will not stack up against his knowledge of the river that you are fishing and the fish that inhabit those waters.

If we take this seriously, I believe it will greatly affect how we view the church. Many people (pastors included) see the church as an aquarium. An aquarium church is a place where Jesus puts all the fish that *he* catches, and we just sort of swim around together, sometimes admiring one another, sometimes bumping into each other—

and sometimes, in the case of piranha Christians, eating one another. But the church is not an aquarium. The church is a charter fishing boat. We are the ones who have signed on to go fishing. And Jesus is the fish finder. Just as Jesus found the fish for Simon and his friends, he will direct us to where the "people fish" are.

Do you believe that Jesus knows where the fish are? Do you believe that he will show *you* where to find them?

Do you dare ask him to take you there?

:: WHEN THE MAGIC IS RIGHT ::

For everything there is a season, and a time
for every matter under heaven. —Ecclesiastes 3:1

I was standing knee deep in the West Branch of the Delaware River, watching trout quietly sipping bugs from the surface of the water a few yards from me. As gently as I could, I cast my fly across the water, where it landed right in the middle of the feeding frenzy. One trout came to the surface and sipped at my fly. It was exciting to see. Just at that moment, though, I was distracted by a splash right at my feet, and I looked down. My reel had fallen off the rod and into the water! When I looked up again, the fish was gone. It would have been the first fish of the vacation; instead it was the first to get away.

A few days later, Ed and I were standing across the river from each other at the Beaver Kill, a historic fly-fishing stream near Roscoe, New York. From his side, Ed could see a large brown trout lying on the bottom near him. Both of us watched a few small fry dimpling the surface. It was just beginning to rain, which was a lucky break, because fish tend to get active during a change in the weather. I took aim and carefully cast a tiny blue-winged olive across the stream to the place Ed pointed out. I couldn't see the trout lying on the bottom, but I saw it begin to ascend, and then glide up and snatch my fly. That one didn't get away. It's a beautiful moment embedded forever in the video library of my mind. When the fishing is slow, I often replay that moment.

In fishing, and often in ministry, timing is everything. The New Testament has a wonderful word that describes this: *kairos*. It is God's time, as opposed to any old time; meaningful time, as opposed to the time that just keeps pacing up and down the hall, or that dogs our footsteps. *Kairos* is time that stands outside of time and intersects with the time in which we live. *Kairos* is time that is invested with meaning that goes far beyond itself. It's the time when it all falls together. In an old television show, The *A-Team*, one of the protagonists used to say, "I love it when a plan comes together." So does God. God loves it so much, someone once said, that God sent the only Son. Or another famous line applies: "All things work together for good for those who love God, who are called according to his purpose" (Romans 8:28).

Very often, *kairos* comes to us in the midst of some of life's most painful events: a death or other loss, a difficult realization, an agonizing decision. It doesn't always feel good, but kairos always is good because it is clothed with the grace of God. And it is good because if we move with it, it will always lead us forward.

There are those times, though, when *kairos* feels like a touch of magic. In ministry, as in fishing, there are those moments when it all falls together. So many of us spend so much of our time sloshing around up to our armpits in trouble (other people's and our own), conflict, and just plain busyness, that we may despair of things ever coming together just right. And then, the magic happens.

For me, the magic moment in fishing is that instant flash when the fish grabs (or even grabs *at*) the fly. Gotcha! Even if I don't land that fish, I feel a surge of accomplishment. I've matched the hatch, the fish has noticed my fly and the action has begun. In ministry, my favorite moments are usually beginnings—times when God is obviously beginning a work in someone's life, or the life of the church; when people are beginning to respond, beginning to reach out, beginning to risk. At these moments, the end is still a long way off

(I may or may not land this "fish"), but the action itself is a sign of grace and God's involvement.

After spending several years being "midwives" to the birth of a new church that seemed like it would never grow beyond its initial growth spurt of seventy-five or so members, we decided to make some changes—among them, a new worship service. Since our existing music staff was not interested in playing for the new service, we considered alternatives. Someone suggested that we start a worship band to attract some new people. We sent people out networking to see if they could find someone who could be the leader of such a band. One couple said they knew someone who might be interested. They invited her to church to "check us out." She came, bringing several friends with her. Over several weeks' time, during the season that would otherwise have been the summer slump, there was an influx of new attenders. The worship band that she now leads has been a significant addition to our ministry.

During that same summer, I was teaching a confirmation class— we call it "Stargazing 101 for Youth." I have a sort of love/hate relationship with confirmation classes. While I enjoy working with the kids and I want Christ to make a difference in their lives, I wonder how much really sinks in, especially when so many of them disappear right after they join the church. I'll never forget a personal conversation that I had with Bobby last summer, though. I was talking to him about what it meant to be a Christian and how to make a commitment to Christ. I asked Bobby if he was ready to make that commitment. He nodded eagerly. "Yes, that's exactly what I'm here for," he said. We prayed together, and for me at least, it was a powerful prayer, knowing that he was one sincere follower of Christ at that very moment. And I know the angels rejoiced that night.

A similar thing happened with us in regard to property. Usually, Presbyterians buy property, and then start the new church. In our case, the initial purchase of property didn't pan out, but the Presbytery called us anyway, and we started collecting people. For six years, as we developed the congregation, we worked with the presbytery and the town to find the right piece of property. That story itself would fill a couple of volumes of conflict manuals and political-intrigue novels. The point is that we would make some headway, but never made it all the way down the river. This year, something different was in the air. We commissioned one of our elders to take over the project. He was "new blood" and not tainted by the conflicts and frustrations of the past. After some long discussions and planning, he proposed a piece of property that was in the right location, with good access from the Garden State Parkway, our major access to the rest of New Jersey. At every step of the way, doors opened. And suddenly, we are owners of twelve acres. We are designing a building, stumping for funds. The congregation is still in shock.

:: HOOK, LINE, AND SINKER ::

Like good stewards of the manifold grace of God,
serve one another with whatever gift each of you has received.
—1 Peter 4:10

In the tackle box of ministry, everyone wants to be the fly. Especially a dry fly, dancing in the surface film, making fish drool and onlookers turn green. The fly, it seems, is where the action is. After all, it is the fly that both attracts and hooks the fish. Those who are most visible, charismatic, and popular may seem to be more vital to the church.

But the fly is attached to the tippet, which is attached to the leader, which is attached to the line, which is attached to the backing, which is wound around the reel, which is firmly bound to the rod. Guides on the length of the rod keep the line from flying off. All are necessary for catching fish. To paraphrase a famous theologian, "If the reel would say, 'Because I am not a fly, I do not belong to the fishing gear,' that would not make it any less a part of the fishing gear. If the whole outfit were a fly, where would the reeling be? If the whole outfit were a leader, where would the netting be? As it is, the Fisher arranged the various pieces of equipment, each one of them, as she chose" (see 1 Corinthians 12:14–26).

Sometimes I am envious of my husband's abilities. He is such a good counselor. He is great at responding to pastoral emergencies. And he is unafraid of working with violent people. I, on the other hand, tend toward teaching and administration, and working with processes. I like speaking at retreats and seminars, and writing. The things that I am best at require a lot of preplanning and quiet time. Which one of us is better at ministry? Well, we both contribute to the total. And each person, in every church, who hears the call to follow Jesus and become involved in the fishing ministry, will have a particular function that will also contribute to the total effectiveness of the church's fishing. No one is any less important than anyone else. Just think of the little guides on the length of the rod. They are not what people usually notice. But remove them from the rod, and the line is uncontrollable, and so is the fly. Each one's ministry is vital. Each one's gifts are uniquely needed by the Fisher, whose hand holds the rod.

:: LEAVE THE DOGS IN THE CABIN ::

And immediately they left their nets and followed him.
—Mark 1:18

One of the best things about our annual fishing trip is that we get to take our Labradors with us. The resort we go to is very "dog friendly," and the cabin is big enough to accommodate the whole herd. They love it when the truck is loaded with fishing gear and they get to hop in and settle down for the ride. When we get there, the first thing they want to do is jump in the river. Being water dogs by nature, they love to swim and play. I love to see them enjoying the outdoors and getting much-needed exercise.

Sometimes the toughest thing that I do when I get suited up to go fishing is to leave the dogs in the cabin. They would love to walk along with me. But Labradors and fly fishing are not a good mix— not if you want to actually catch fish. Fish are skittish, and will bolt at any unnatural disturbance in the water. Besides which, having a panting dog by your side tends to negatively influence your ability to concentrate on the task. At least it does for me. Maybe your Lab will sit quietly on the bank while you're fishing. Mine won't.

The point of course, is that we can't do everything at once. We have to make choices, and with every road taken, another is left behind. If fishing is a priority, then some other things will need to be left behind in order to fish effectively.

That was Jesus' point when he suggested to a wealthy young man that if he wanted to follow him, he'd best get rid of his encumbrances (Matthew 19:21). There are times in our life when we would do well to take a good hard look at the things that are standing in the way of our ministry.

It's interesting that the fishermen disciples had to leave their fishing in order to go fishing.

Does your desire for a comfortable lifestyle keep you from accepting a call to a place where money is tight? Does your need to be liked keep you from challenging oppressive structures and injustice? Do you have habitual behaviors or attitudes that spook the fish? Is change difficult for you to accept? Are you hiding an addiction that keeps you from being free in your ministry? Are you so attached to your particular work that you can't see beyond it to the call of Christ? It's interesting that the fishermen disciples had to *leave* their fishing in order to *go* fishing. Which just goes to prove that you can't make following Christ into a formula. Your call is as unique as you are. So are the roadblocks standing in the way.

Like Peter (who was agitated by Jesus' conversation with the wealthy young man), we may be all too aware of what we have left behind: "Look, we have left everything and followed you. What then will we have?" (Matthew 19:27). (Translation: "Are we doing this for nothing?") Jesus does not leave him guessing: "When the Son of Man is seated on the throne of his glory, you who have followed me will also sit on twelve thrones, judging the twelve tribes of Israel. And everyone who has left houses or brothers or sisters or father or mother or children or fields, for my name's sake, will receive a hundredfold, and will inherit eternal life" (Matthew 19:28–29).

This business of "leaving behind" is not just a physical exercise. In many ways, the emotional leaving is more difficult, and more important, than the physical. We can leave any number of things behind while still being attached to them emotionally. And that emotional attachment can be a hindrance to our ministry.

When I first went off to seminary, I left home, family, and everything that was familiar. It felt like tearing flesh from a wound. And it took me years to recover. My new life was so different, and I felt so vulnerable. Yet, God was there, and God led me on.

What I have discovered since then is that such "leaving behind" is not a once-for-all kind of thing. Having once left it all behind, we begin to accumulate things, relationships, and securities all over again. If we have not learned to hold on to them lightly, some of them may start to get in the way of our fishing. Just like the Labs by the side of the stream.

:: ILLUSION ::

"Woe to you, scribes and Pharisees, hypocrites!
For you are like whitewashed tombs,
which on the outside look beautiful,
but inside they are full of the bones of the dead
and of all kinds of filth." —Matthew 23:27

When all is said and done, the art of fly fishing is the art of illusion. The intent of the fly fisher, while tying flies, while reading the water,

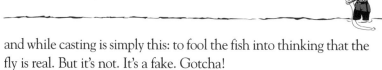

and while casting is simply this: to fool the fish into thinking that the fly is real. But it's not. It's a fake. Gotcha!

Here is where my metaphor must of necessity break down. It's all too easy in this life to put on a façade in our personal life and in the life of the church. To say to others, in essence, "This is how I want you to experience me, but it isn't real. The real me is somewhere deep below the surface, where you'll never find me. Or, if you do find me, you'll be sorely disappointed." Put a couple hundred façades in one room together, and you get a congregation with a false front. It looks nice enough on the outside, but there's no substance within.

It's humorous sometimes to watch a fish come up to a perfectly good fly and swim around it, even bump it with its nose, or sip it lightly to get a taste, and then soundly reject it. Fish are not always subtle in turning down an invitation to lunch! They're very sensitive to a fake.

Our "fish" out in our communities are sensitive too. People today value authenticity. They don't care what you *say* you believe. They care about what you *do*. Another way to say it is that people are quick to spot your core values. There are lots of things that we say we value, but our core values are the values that we actually live by. Churches are famous for having mission statements that don't connect with their real core values. They say they want to attract young families, but the nursery is moldy, with broken-down cribs. They say they want to try new things, but instead, they cut the budget. They say they want to help people meet Jesus, but when newcomers come through the door, they get the cold shoulder instead of the handshake of peace.

When we go fishing for people, we cannot deliver a false product. It's got to be the real thing.

4 :: WISDOM FROM THE RIVER

There is a river whose streams
make glad the city of God.
—Psalm 46:4a

:: THERE IS A RIVER ::

IT'S BECOME A HABIT for Ed and me to take a two-week fishing vacation every year, usually in September. It fits us, not just because of the fishing, but because a fishing resort is a place where we can also take our Labradors and have a quiet time in a natural setting, getting back in touch with ourselves, each other, and the river. It's a kind of Sabbath, one that we keep as religiously as our morning prayer time and our weekly day off.

The two weeks have a rhythm of their own, governed by the river and rest. Once we have unloaded the truck and settled into the cabin, time seems suspended. Days go by, but there is no rush, no deadlines. I feel as if I've stepped into eternity. The world of work and worry seems far away, and God is very present. And while I am there, God does the restorative work that my soul needs.

I am always weary when I go to the river, often stressed and pushed, sometimes a little chewed around the edges. Can you relate? These are tough times for those of us who are in ministry. When I read Paul's words to Timothy about "distressing times" to come—times marked by selfishness, arrogance, abuse, treachery, pleasure-seeking, and the like, and resulting in a kind of "godliness" that looks good on the outside but is devoid of power—I think, "Yes, this is the time" (see 2 Timothy 3:1–5). We live in a world that is, at best, apathetic to the work of the church. Many are in congregations rife with conflict. Pastors and people are often at odds, with more and more pastors either burning out or acting out. The world about us is violent and often frightening. Then, there are those life issues that we face, just like everyone else: health concerns, family concerns, aging parents, decisions and dilemmas. In the midst of it all, we often wonder whether our ministry is making a difference at all.

And that's why Ed and I go to the river—to regain our perspective so that we can face the world with confidence and peace.

Oddly enough, a busy highway and a set of railroad tracks overlook one of our favorite fishing spots in the Catskills. Cars, semis, and logging trucks roar by. From time to time, a train lumbers past. Still, when I am there fishing, the world melts away. As the dusk settles and a faint mist rises from the water, a chorus of frogs rehearses its anthem. Gentle dimples dot the surface of the water as the trout sip blue-winged olives. The silence is profound, despite the nearness of the working world.

At those times, I am reminded of what the Psalmist said: "There *is* a river that makes glad the city of God." There is a river. The presence of a river is good news for people who live in an arid country such as Israel. The river provides reassurance, comfort, security, nurture. In the next verse, the psalmist brings the point home: "God is in the midst." In other words, God *is* the river. God is our reassurance, our comfort, our security.

These words about the river—God—follow a well-known and often used comment about God being "our refuge and strength, a very present help in trouble." I often use this psalm when talking to people who are going through tough times. I find the words especially meaningful to use in the face of a sudden death. God's presence enables people to face change and tumult and even disaster with the confidence that comes from the knowledge of ultimate security. The psalm is effective for those times, but I believe that it is foundational at all times for those of us who are in ministry. It is a call back to the river, back to the source, back to God, who is "in the midst."

Don't forget: there *is* a river. We are not in this alone. God, who inhabits eternity, will touch our lives in the present day.

As the two weeks of our fishing begin to wind to a close, my inner clock starts ticking again. I begin to think of the tasks that need done, the work left behind. As I step back into the workaday world, I find that I do not leave the river behind, but the river comes with me, in my heart and soul.

Where do you go to restore your soul? Where is that place for you where time can melt away into eternity and God can touch your heart? It need not be far, and it need not be a lonely place. But it must *be*. And you must go there, daily, weekly, yearly—whatever kind of rhythm works for you—for the health and sustenance of your soul.

I know, I know—there is much to be done, people need you. But it's okay. God will take care of the world while you're away. And when you come back, you won't be alone.

:: REALITY CHECK ::

As they were going along the road, someone said to him,
"I will follow you wherever you go." And Jesus said to him,
"Foxes have holes, and birds of the air have nests;
but the Son of Man has nowhere to lay his head."
—Luke 9:57–58

When I think about fishing, the images that come into my mind are pleasant ones: the sun is shining, with a few clouds to keep it from getting too hot, the river placidly flowing over rocks and around bends, trout feeding noisily on a cloud of caddis flies while I make graceful casts in their midst. Just as the fly reaches the surface of the water, a hefty trout pokes a nose out of the water and grabs it, and the fight begins. The fish dances across the river to greet me, and I scoop it out of the water and gently send it back to its watery home.

The reality of fishing is usually much different from my fantasy. The weather is less than perfect—pouring rain or beating sun—and the fish have gone into hiding. My casting is rusty because I haven't been fishing for a while. The wind comes up. Pretty soon, I have a snarl in my leader the size of Connecticut. For the next fifteen minutes, I patiently stand and pick at the leader, while on the opposite bank the fish miraculously decide it's time to start feeding. By the time I've unsnarled the leader, the fish have finished their dessert and gone down for a nap.

The reality of fishing is usually much different from my fantasy.

When Ed and I went fishing with a guide last spring, we anticipated a great fishing day. It started out mediocre: overcast (a good thing for the flies), but windy (not a good thing). As we drifted down the river, the day went from mediocre to bad to worse, from windy to rainy to lightning, thunder, and hail. Feeding fish were few and far between. The cabin was at the halfway point, and we stopped to grab a snack and to let the dogs out. Then we got back in the drift boat to try again. More rain and wind, and just a few rising trout. During one of the rain showers, the guide turned to me and said, "Most women think we guys are crazy for doing things like this." I shrugged and said, "I'm different." I don't mind getting a little wet or cold in the pursuit of the big one.

The point is this: anglers willingly spend a whole lot of their time doing things other than casting flies and reeling in fish. A whole lot of that time is spent in battling inclement weather and fixing things. It's not unlike other activities. We watch a football game to see the snap, the pass, the tackle, and the touchdown, but more time is spent

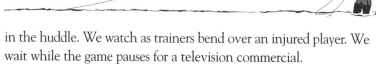

in the huddle. We watch as trainers bend over an injured player. We wait while the game pauses for a television commercial.

Ministry is much the same. There are many images in our minds about what is "fun" about ministry. For me, it's being in front of a congregation, preaching or teaching. It's seeing the organization of leaders and ministries functioning effectively. It's watching as people make significant spiritual commitments and grow in leadership. But a whole lot of my time is spent on other things: untangling miscommunication, repairing relationships, listening to problems, sitting with groups as they struggle through tough decisions.

I'm in the middle of a "writing week" right now. But Monday night I had a funeral, and Tuesday afternoon and evening were taken up with conversations with people in two of the churches that I'm currently working with because of my Committee on Ministry responsibilities for presbytery. This morning, it was more of the same.

I complained to someone, "I'm not supposed to be doing this stuff, I'm supposed to be writing!"

"You want me to feel sorry for you?" he asked with a chuckle. "I just had to give up three days of my vacation for this stuff."

After I had been in the ministry about a year, during a period when I was feeling more of the struggle than the victory of ministry, someone I barely knew (and who was not in "the" ministry) said effusively, "Isn't being in the ministry wonderful?" I don't remember what I replied, but I remember what I was thinking: "You've got to be kidding! You don't know beans about the ministry. It's pain, struggle, and failure. Get real."

The ministry is not a profession to enter lightly. Your line *will* get tangled, and you *will* run into bad weather. Without a strong dose of realism, a budding young pastor may fall into discouragement and doubt. Yet, there is great hope, and that is what keeps us fishing in the midst of the tangle. The fish are out there. We know it. We can feel it in our bones.

"Therefore, since it is by God's mercy that we are engaged in this ministry, we do not lose heart" (2 Corinthians 4:1).

62   :: HAZARDS ::

But we have this treasure in clay jars, so that it may be made clear that this extraordinary power belongs to God and does not come from us. —2 Corinthians 4:7

It was a size twenty-two blue-winged olive, tied loop-wing style.[1] A beautiful little specimen, almost guaranteed to catch fish. And it was lodged securely in my husband's finger. He had been rigging up a brand new rod and reel—a ritual any angler enjoys. He unwound a leader and tied it to the end of the fly line. To extend the life of the leader, he tied on a length of the tippet material and then the crowning glory, the fly. But in spite of his eagerness, it wasn't his night. The leader slipped and the hook engaged his tender flesh. It might have been easier to dislodge had he squeezed down the barb ahead of time. But that's the problem. If we saw the future ahead of time, we could avoid lots of trouble. But usually we don't.

It was not a great injury. No stitches or band-aids were required. Some first-aid cream would fix the finger, and time would heal his bruised ego. Still, it was a painful enough reminder that every sport has its hazards, and many of them hit when you least expect them to.

And so it is with ministry. There will be wounds great and small. Not just for those in high-risk ministry—the mission field, the inner city—but also in "safe" suburbia. These days, ministry is a most hazardous undertaking. Our culture is, at best, indifferent to the church. Church people themselves can be cold and demanding and cantankerous. The sources of stress and temptation are legion. In many and varied ways we experience being vulnerable "clay jars" that hold the treasure called ministry.

I've often thought it would be nice to be something other than human in the midst of ministry. Being human is so very vulnerable.

---

1. *A blue-winged olive is a type of fly. It can be tied in many styles, including "parachute," "loop wing," or "comparadun."*

Human beings are vulnerable to physical limitations, illness, injury, and death, vulnerable to the wagging tongues of the gossips and to our own weakness.

What is amazing to me is that significant ministry often happens in spite of—in the midst of—being so very human. A colleague was caught in a misdeed, and he paid for that misdeed in the courts of the church. Supported by his wife and congregation, he faced his issues, "did his time," and returned to his ministry. Even in the midst of the struggle, the church grew. Why? I suspect that God was there somewhere.

:: MURPHY'S LAW OF FISHING ::

Peter answered him, "Lord, if it is you,
command me to come to you on the water."
He said, "Come." So Peter got out of the boat,
started walking on the water, and came toward Jesus.
But when he noticed the strong wind, he became frightened,
and beginning to sink, he cried out, "Lord, save me!"
Jesus immediately reached out his hand and caught him,
saying to him, "You of little faith, why did you doubt?"
—Matthew 14:28–31

People in churches like to talk about the "good old days." "Remember when we had two hundred kids in Sunday school every week, Martha? Boy, howdy, that was when we had seventy-five in the youth group, too." Now, of course, there are barely twenty-five in both combined, and that's if you count the preacher's dog. But that young upstart preacher down the street has kids hanging out the doors, and a full house every Sunday morning.

If you are hung up on numbers (let's be honest: what preacher isn't?), Murphy's Law can get you every time. You're likely to be one

64 step behind or one step ahead of the next big wave. If only the conditions were different, then we'd be making progress. But that can't happen now, not the way things are.

Murphy's Law is often in operation when I'm fishing, too. Here's how I experience it:

1. Fishing was great yesterday. (It will probably be better tomorrow.)
2. The fish are always rising on the other side of the stream. (It's too deep to wade there.)
3. If you go across the stream toward the rising fish, a fish will jump right where you were standing. (You'll never get back there in time.)
4. The least-experienced angler always catches the biggest fish. (Unless *you* happen to be the least experienced.)
5. Fish always start rising when you are changing your leader. Even more rise if you have a snarl in your line. (Climb up on the bank to work on your snarl, and there'll be a feeding frenzy.)

In both fishing and ministry, Murphy's Law is often simply a matter of externalizing blame. "It's not my fault I didn't catch any fish. The weather was lousy." (Translation: "I spent the whole vacation sitting in front of the fire with my feet up.") "I can't help it that Sunday attendance is dropping; look at all the soccer games they are playing now." (Translation: "I expect the fish to come to me.")

For a whole lot of us, it's time to stop whining about the rotten conditions and to start believing that God is at work, whether we can see the evidence or not—even more so if we *do* see the evidence.

Many times, we think we are afraid of failure. But as our old friend Peter can attest, success can sometimes be far more frightening. When he was standing on top of those slippery waves on a stormy night, he knew it shouldn't be happening. Nobody can walk on water! Yet, that was precisely what he was doing. Then something went wrong. No, he didn't trip. He didn't forget his lines. He simply stopped believing. This walk on the water couldn't possibly be happening. So, all of a sudden, it wasn't.

Sure, it's good to be realistic. If something can go wrong, it may

well go wrong. It's good to be ready. But let's not be so ready for things
to go wrong that we miss out on what God is doing.

:: INDEPENDENCE ::

Jesus went on with his disciples to the villages of
Caesarea Philippi; and on the way he asked his disciples,
"Who do people say that I am?" And they answered him,
"John the Baptist; and others, Elijah; and still others,
one of the prophets." He asked them,
"But who do you say that I am?"
Peter answered him, "You are the Messiah."
—Mark 8:27–29

My fly-fishing idol is Joan Wulff, who is without question the best fly
fisherwoman in the world, and who can outfish most men. In her
book, *Fly Fishing*, she talks about the importance of women becoming
independent in their fishing. "We can get more and give more," she
says, "by being independent and by making decisions and being comfortable with them."[2] To illustrate, she describes the experience of a
friend who was dating a man who was a more experienced fisher.

> He caught the first fish. She asked what he was
> using. He told her. She put that fly on. They continued
> fishing. She saw him catch more fish while she was shut
> out. Half an hour later she complained that the fly
> hadn't worked for her. His reply: "Oh, they stopped tak-
> ing that fly and I changed to such and such." This kind
> of experience (which I have had) makes you feel frus-
> trated. Being dependent can freeze you in the learning

---

2. Joan Wulff, Fly Fishing: Expert Advice from a Woman's Perspective *(Harrisburg,
Pa.: Stackpole Books, 1991)*, 82.

process. If you never take the responsibility, you never get the reward. Don't fall into this trap!

Fishing alone changes this. You have no one to answer to except yourself, and your competition is with the fish. You will be more aware; you'll think more "like a fish" when left to your own devices. You'll be building your own knowledge, one step at a time, knowing what you did that worked, not what someone else did. There is more than one way to catch a trout and you'll find it. Fishing alone will do a lot for you.[3]

A similar thing holds true in ministry. It's easy to be awed by the "experts" in various fields. And it's tempting to want to follow the jot and tittle of their method. But if you were to dig into the history of those "experts," no doubt you will find that they became good at what they do not because they merely copied someone else, but because they learned, through prayer and study and observation, how to effectively reach people. As is true in trout fishing, there are also many ways to "catch people." Some of those ways will be more fitting to my gifts and personality, and others may be more workable for you. And each "stream" where we do ministry is different.

My husband is a "late bloomer" in ministry, having started seminary at age forty-two. Though I am considerably younger than he, I am his senior in ministry experience. I respect his gifts and his life experience, which from the beginning made him a great counselor and able to relate to people from all walks of life. I have no problem deferring to his greater wisdom in his areas of giftedness and experience (nor does he have any difficulty deferring to mine in the same way). I complained at first, though, when he decided to go into the ministry, and balked initially at the idea of serving together. "People will naturally assume that you are the minister," I said. And there have been many times over the years that this has

---

3. Joan Wulff, *Fly Fishing: Expert Advice from a Woman's Perspective* (*Harrisburg, Pa.: Stackpole Books, 1991*), 82.

happened. But what troubles me more is my own tendency to defer. From time to time, I have caught myself deferring to him in areas where I am more gifted or more experienced, or where I feel a strong conviction in one direction or another. Why? Because he is a man and I am a woman? Because he is older, and therefore more experienced in life?

This is not just a male/female issue, nor is it about age. It's about learning to trust one's own instincts. It's about learning responsibility in ministry and being willing to stand by what you decide. Ed and I have served as co-pastors for about fifteen years and have learned a great deal from each other. For the past year, though, we have been serving in separate ministries, for the first time since he was ordained. It has not been surprising that we've missed each other's presence at some key points. We've learned to trust each other's instincts and have valued each other's strengths. What *has* been surprising is how much each of has grown in the brief time we've been working separately. It's been an enlightening experience for both of us as we've discovered (rediscovered) some of our own strengths and weaknesses. We discovered the areas where we tended to "hide" behind each other. The experience has stretched us in ways neither of us expected, and we've grown in confidence and leadership.

This is not just a male/female issue, nor is it about age. It's about learning to trust one's own instincts.

Beyond our spouse, there are other potential areas where we may need to learn a greater independence and responsibility. When we moved to New Jersey to start a new church, we were told by our presbytery that a phone campaign was to be the fishing method in landing the core group for our church. Phone solicitors have been around for a long time, and we were not eager to use the method. In the past, my husband had operated a "boiler room" to sell advertising, so he knew both the hazards and the potentials. We were aware that a number of churches had started successfully using this method, but we seriously wondered whether the window was closing on people's tolerance level. It was also a concern when we learned that more than one local church had recently used phone campaigns with only minimal success. Still, the presbytery had "cut the bait," and it was our turn to fish. So we did, to miserable results (I should qualify that by saying that all of the dozen or so "fish" that we caught by this method made wonderful members; but it just didn't seem to be cost- or energy-effective, nor did it give us the "quick start" that was intended).

Now, don't stop attending conferences and continuing-education events. And don't stop talking to the folks in your higher judicatories. And please don't stop being a good partner with your spouse. The willingness to learn from others and work cooperatively with others is a sign of maturity and provides a great avenue for growth. But we should never rely *solely* on the advice or methods of other people. We need to learn to make our own decisions and stand by them. We need to learn from some of our own mistakes as well as from our successes. We each stand before God and must answer to God as to how we have used our own gifts and how we have responded to God's call in our life.

:: ONE SIZE DOES NOT FIT ALL ::

There is no longer Jew or Greek, there is no longer slave or free, there is no longer male and female; for all of you are one in Christ Jesus. —Galatians 3:28

On my Christmas list last year was a new fly-fishing vest. Ed had been telling me for years that I needed a new one, and I knew he was right. The instant I put on the new vest, I could tell a significant difference. This vest fit me! My old vest was a men's small, which for me was still pretty baggy. But it was all they had back when I started fly fishing. And I made do. And when I bought my first neoprene waders, they, too, were a men's small. That's what happens when you enter a sport that has mostly been practiced by the gender not your own.

So, too, with ministry. I remember guest preaching at a large church early in my ministry. It was a colonial-style sanctuary, with ominously large chairs sitting behind the pulpit. I remember trying to sit down in one of the colonial white chairs with red cushions. If I sat all the way back, my legs went straight out in front of me, because the seat was too long. If I sat forward so my knees could bend, my feet still dangled above the floor. I must have arrived in Brobdingnag, or perhaps I was caught in a *Twilight Zone* episode, "The Incredible Shrinking Preacher." At any rate, it was far from comfortable. I was glad when I got to get up and preach—though I didn't fit the pulpit any better than I fit the chairs. In my own church, they had fitted me with a nice wooden box to stand on, so that I wouldn't look like a little old lady driving a Cadillac.

In fishing, as in ministry, one size does not fit all. And when women began infiltrating both the sport and the profession, this fact began to be painfully obvious. The church was "built" around male leadership. And many people (including women) wanted it to stay that way. In my early years of ministry, though, it wasn't other people's comfort level that bothered me so much as my own. Being unassertive by nature, brought up in a conservative family and trained in an even more conservative theological position in my college Christian fellowship, I did not enter the ministry with a flaming feminist perspective. Truth be known, I entered seminary thinking that women didn't belong in the ministry (but what does one do when confronted by God's call?). At a banquet during orientation week, a male student just made it worse when he accosted me with his theology and said I ought to go home. When I graduated, my feelings were still mixed. Still, I had come to know that God was calling me into the ministry. So I went forward, trusting that God would somehow show me the way. I had the youthful innocence to believe that if God called me to be a pastor, then God would find me a church to serve in.

My first call out of seminary beat some of my nonassertiveness out of me as it challenged me to clarify my theological position. It also proved to me that God does have a sense of humor. I was "Woman Interim Pastor" for the Presbyterian Synod of Alaska-Northwest. My day job was to serve as an interim pastor, and then I was to moonlight as a women's advocacy speaker for various groups and churches within the synod. The job was a Godsend—literally. Having gone to seminary with a strong sense of call, but a conflicting theology, I was forced back into the Scriptures to find out whether God was going against God's own Word by calling me! I made it clear in an interview for the synod paper that my agenda would not be "women's issues" but the proclamation of the gospel. A female clergy colleague (more on the feminist edge than I was) had me for lunch over that comment!

As I studied the Bible and opened my eyes to what Jesus and others in the New Testament (even Paul!) were doing in regard to the ministry of women, I began to understand that a part of the gospel message is that women are full participants in God's kingdom, and that includes ministry. As I have become comfortable with both the theology and my own leadership in ministry, I have felt less "battered" by zealots on either extreme of the feminist-chauvinist continuum.

My new fishing vest is a women's small. So are my new wading jacket and my breathable waders. They seem a little strange, because I got used to the baggy look. Even so, it makes me feel good, because I am being recognized as both a woman and an angler. A similar thing has happened in ministry. As the years have passed, more women have come on the ministry scene. And the church has begun to accommodate. Vestment catalogues now have several styles of robes cut for women. Women are present at every level of church government. After over twenty years in the ministry, I still watch for a look of surprise when I mention to someone that I'm a pastor. More often now, I'm the one who is surprised, because there is no surprise on the other person's face.

:: FISHING WITH A GUIDE (PART 1) ::   71

What then is Apollos? What is Paul? Servants through whom you
came to believe, as the Lord assigned to each. I planted,
Apollos watered, but God gave the growth. —1 Corinthians 3:5–6

We've wanted to do it for years. But it seemed too much of a luxury.
It was enough of a struggle to scrape together enough money to cover the cost of the cabin and flies, much less a guide. Every time we
would go to the river, though, we would talk about it. Maybe this is
the time. Could we afford it? The mystique about it, of course, is that
the guide knows where the fish are. We sometimes know where the
fish are, but then again, very often we don't. And the guide also
knows what flies to use. We often guess—wrong. My fantasy was that
if we took just one trip with a guide, it would do two things for us.
First, it would assure us of at least one day of catching fish, and second, from then on, we'd be privy to the secrets of the West Branch
of the Delaware River.

Last year we finally broke down and hired a guide named John
to take us on a float trip down the river. His job, he said, was to get
us where the fish were and to teach us some new techniques.

He helped me get serious about learning the "reach cast," and
confirmed that my basic cast needed some serious work. (See "The
Cast," in chapter 3.)

He also taught me that even guides get skunked sometimes. The
day we went fishing with John started out cloudy. A good sign, John
said. Then it progressed to rainy and windy. Not so good, John said.
And it made his work all the harder. Instead of just guiding the boat
downstream with the oars, John was forced to row most of the time,
fighting against the wind. There weren't many observable hatches
that day, and only a few good rises. As we neared the halfway point
stopover at our cabin, the rain and wind gave way to lightning, thunder, and hail. I didn't catch a thing all day.

The moral of the story? Even the best guide can't guarantee that

72 you'll catch fish. To quote an expert in a different field: "I planted, Apollos watered, but God gave the growth" (1 Corinthians 3:6).

:: FISHING WITH A GUIDE (PART 2) ::

"But you will receive power when the Holy Spirit has come upon you; and you will be my witnesses in Jerusalem, in all Judea and Samaria, and to the ends of the earth." —Acts 1:8

Generally speaking, I'm the kind of person who can be happy fishing my little section of the river. I know where the fish usually are rising—if they're rising—and I can be content walking back and forth between my favorite holes, watching and waiting for some action. When John took us fishing in his drift boat, it became clear that getting out on the river in a boat creates lots more options. You can cover more of the river, and even on a bad day (it was), you can move from a no-fish spot to other spots along the river where there may be some action. It won't guarantee that you'll catch fish, but it will give you more opportunities to try.

It's easy for both pastors and congregations to become a little too ingrown. In some churches it seems like someone has installed one of those invisible electrified fences around the church building. No one feels safe moving out beyond that line. That boundary is where ministry takes place. Period. People are content to walk along in their familiar routes and do their familiar little jobs, and wait for the fish to come to them.

What would it take to pry your congregation loose from their pews and get them out in the river? Maybe some home repair projects? Work at a soup kitchen? Our congregation likes to have a booth at our county fair. Another congregation we know does an annual project called "Paint Your Heart Out," in which church members go out and paint several homes for people in need, all on one Saturday in a given year. It doesn't cost a lot of money, but it does cost some time and it stretches the comfort zone.

We need to get out there on the river, where the fish are—and not just the fish we already know.

:: FISHING WITH A GUIDE (PART 3) ::

The eye cannot say to the hand, "I have no need of you,"
nor again the head to the feet, "I have no need of you."
—*1 Corinthians 12:21*

One of the dangers in the ministry (especially, I think, for a couple in ministry together) is the illusion of self-sufficiency. Coupled with that is a spiritual trap that says, "God is all-sufficient" (well, God is), so God and I should be able to handle anything. The reality is that despite our giftedness, and despite God's power and accessibility, we still need others in the body of Christ. Our pride may make it difficult to accept, but we don't know everything about the river or the fish that swim there. Sometimes we need help. Church leaders who are wise will recognize that accepting the help of a guide shows strength not weakness. The guide may be a friend or mentor, a counselor or spiritual director—perhaps a consultant or a denominational representative, someone with a particular expertise or insight who can help us navigate difficult waters or handle prickly fish.

Fishing with a guide requires a couple of things: the willingness to learn, along with the acceptance of our own limitations.

The best experience I've had with a guide in a church situation was when Ed and I were serving a church as interim pastors. The congregation was full of great people who couldn't get along with each other. In fact, they really couldn't communicate. Third-party conversations were the norm. They had just lost a pastor through conflict and were smarting from the experience. After we had identified some of the issues, we called in a consultant who helped the session and congregation renegotiate some of their rules for communication. In a nutshell, the result was that they agreed to communicate directly instead of indirectly. (One of those "one small step for a man, one giant leap for mankind" decisions.)

:: THE RIGHT RESORT FOR ME ::

Do not neglect to show hospitality to strangers, for by doing that some have entertained angels without knowing it. —Hebrews 13:2

We were exploring the area for a new place to go fishing and decided to stay in a little cabin that we heard about at a fly-fishing show. The resort was owned by a well-known fly fishing expert. The minute we drove up to the "cabin," I was disappointed. Granted, it was right on the banks of the river (the dogs were ecstatic), but it was just a dumpy little trailer. We had to bring our own cooking utensils. There was no television. It was just one outer room, with a teeny-tiny bedroom with a double bed that barely cleared the walls. Now mind you, I have stayed in some fairly rustic cabins in my life. Some of the best vacations of our marriage were spent in cheap log cabins with mile-wide cracks between the logs. But, well, maybe I'm just getting older. I wanted some creature comforts. It was a very chilly late September, and the heater didn't work. Even the dogs were cold. Spike (who, by the way, weighs one hundred pounds) climbed on the bed every night and plopped on top of the bed right between us, pushing me ever closer toward the small crack between the wall and the bed and making me fight for covers. We had reservations to stay two weeks, so I tried to settle in. But I just couldn't. Don't get me wrong. The river was great, and the fish were there. But I just wasn't comfortable.

For the first time ever, I asked Ed if we could go home a couple of days early. We did.

What made the whole experience worse was that every time we talked to one of the people who worked at the resort, they were grousing about the resort down the road that had done such terrible things. *They* had a fly shop out by the main road that was in direct competition with the place we were staying. *Their* guides were terrible. *They* catered to vacationers, not real anglers. *They* kept on building new cabins, polluting the environment. *They* were even rumored (this is anathema) to plant fish where visitors couldn't help but catch them—right in front of their cabins.

Whoa! For a minute there, I thought I was back in church. One particular church we served pops into my mind, one that had an *attitude*, if you know what I mean. They always kept talking about that church down the street that had taken away some of their members—*and* their money—and had done a host of other awful things.

The more the resort people talked about that *other* resort, the more we wanted to see it. The day before we left, we finally drove down the road and paid it a visit. Within an hour, we had taken a tour of the cabins and made a reservation for the following year. It was obvious from the get-go that they cared about their customers. The heaters worked. There were even microwave ovens and cooking utensils in the cabins. Fireplaces. Need I go on? Yes, it cost a little bit more, but I happily put aside the extra money during the year, just waiting for the chance to come to this resort.

Sometimes, churches make excuses for not providing a few "creature comforts" to make church visitors feel more at home. Sometimes good church folks disguise their jealousy of other churches behind self-righteous statements. They cry, "Poor me!" but very often they are not poor, they are just cheap. They cry, "Foul!" but they themselves are simply without vision. My hunch is that this just makes people want to visit that other church all the more. And more than likely, they will stay once they get there.

76 :: YOU CAN'T CONTROL THE WEATHER ::

*So when they had come together, they asked him, "Lord, is this
the time when you will restore the kingdom to Israel?"
He replied, "It is not for you to know the times or periods that
the Father has set by his own authority. But you will receive
power when the Holy Spirit has come upon you; and you
will be my witnesses in Jerusalem, in all Judea and Samaria,
and to the ends of the earth." —Acts 1:6–8*

We were supposed to have a presbytery meeting today. All day. Once
a month the forty-five churches in our presbytery get together to do
our common work. But New Jersey weather is unpredictable. The
Atlantic Ocean often moderates winter storms along the shore, and
we escape the snow. But not this time. We were socked in. And
everything stopped. On this particular occasion, it felt like a merci-
ful gift. We'd been too busy, too stressed. An enforced break was wel-
come. Besides, you can't control the weather. Might as well enjoy it.

When we go to the river for our annual fishing vacation, people
send us off with wishes for good weather. Usually we say, "It doesn't
matter what the weather is like. It's so great to be by the river that it's
okay if we get some rain." Once in a while, though, things get a little out of hand. On one recent trip, we were visited by the remnants
of Hurricane Floyd. Besides Floyd, there were a several other rain
days. And every time it rained, the ecosystem took some time to settle back down to normal. We still enjoyed being there, but the frustration that I expressed when we left was, "I didn't learn anything."

I really enjoy the learning process that goes on when I'm fishing.
Many of the rivers that we have fished are tough rivers (maybe they
all are). And it's not unusual to go several days without catching all
that much. Even though we tend to go to the same environment at
roughly the same time each year, we can't assume that the same flies
that worked last year will work this time. The environment of the
river changes daily. If the water temperature isn't right, the flies won't

hatch. If it's windy, they won't stay on the water. If the river is higher or lower than normal, the fish will migrate to new spots. If it rains, the water will be muddy for a while, and you might as well forget dry flies.[4] The fish won't see them. After a few days of fishing, though, a pattern usually begins to emerge. And I start catching more fish as I begin to understand the system. Each time, I learn a little more about the fish and the insects that they eat. But when the weather keeps changing, patterns can be tough to discern. And that was my problem in the year that Floyd visited the river. I left with a sense of incompleteness. I didn't learn anything.

If pressed, I suppose I would have to admit that I did learn one thing: you can't control the weather. And it isn't always "natural disasters" that affect the fishing. The stretch of river that we most often fish on the Delaware is controlled by a dam upstream. For reasons of their own, the managers of the dam sometimes let a few extra tons of water over the dam. Or they hold back the normal flow in order to preserve water. In either case, the fish are affected. If the river is higher than usual, there may be more fish available, but they are tougher to find because they are moving around (and the water may be over my waders in the prime fishing spots). If the water is lower than normal, many fish may have left the area in search of deeper pools, and may spook easily because they see the angler coming.

There are patterns that can be discerned in people's lives and in the life of a given church that point to a direction for ministry to take.

In ministry, changes in the ecosystem can be just as frustrating. I've learned quite a bit about people over the years—and about systems and conflict and change. There are patterns that can be discerned in people's lives and in the life of a given church that point to a direction for ministry to take. But sometimes the only discernable pattern is change, or one bad break after another, or one new

---

4. *While there are many types of flies, there are two main categories: dry or wet. Dry flies float on the surface film of the water, while wet flies are designed to submerge.*

78

conflict after another. Sometimes pastors say that they are so busy "putting out fires" that they don't have time to think creatively for the future (denominational executives say it even more often). They leave a parish in disgust or frustration, wishing desperately that they could have done more, or at least learned something that would be useful elsewhere.

That was true for us when we left a church a few years ago. Even when reading the church's information form prior to our call there, we sensed a kind of darkness. When we arrived there to begin our ministry, the most obvious emotion coming from people was anger. As we continued on and began to learn more about the congregation, we unwittingly uncovered some of the church's dark secrets that held the church in its bondage of anger. Neither the church nor the presbytery was willing or ready to face the secrets and deal with them. So, we left, in an unresolved state of mind and heart. But in churches, as in fishing, you can't control the weather. You can just do your best and trust that God will open doors for ministry in God's own time. Sometimes, the best you can hope for is that you touched a few people with the grace of God. Like the Red Cross, you patched up a few souls, and gave them back their lives. Perhaps, like King David, you are not the one to "build the house." But you may build the foundation. Perhaps, in God's time, the muddy water will finally settle out and the feeding frenzy will begin.

:: THE SAME RIVER TWICE ::

"And no one after drinking old wine desires new wine, but says, 'The old is good.'" —Luke 5:39

A friend in Alaska, a Catholic priest (coincidentally, a whale of a good cook), used to tell us that in the Anchorage area it was pointless for the diocese to continually move priests around to different churches. He said that the population of the area was so transitional that over a period of three years, you had a whole new congregation. This was due to the transient populations of two military bases and the oil industry. They moved him anyway.

It's been said that you don't step into the same river twice. The water that was here a few moments ago has already moved on downstream. And there are changes from day to day due to weather and water conditions. One of the great things about a river is that there is the constant sense of movement, yet a very comforting stability. A river is a symbol of trust. The water continues to move; there's more where that came from.

Churches ought to be like that—a sense of movement with a comforting stability. You can't step into the same church twice because it is always changing, yet there is that sense that God, who is same yesterday, today, and forever, continues to pour grace into the lives of God's people.

But in churches it is often the opposite. There's no outward sign of movement, but no real stability either. Conflicts tear the fabric of the congregation; gossip keeps information moving, but holds back the truth. There's a tendency to dam up the resources instead of letting them flow into ministry, trusting that there is more where that came from.

I once read that the only way to keep a fence the same is to change it. If you paint a fence white when you put it up, over years it will begin to fade and show wear. To keep it the same, you have to keep painting it, refreshing it. Many times, churches, in a desire to retain what is good in their ministry, their history, and their experience, find themselves deteriorating. They wonder why, but the answer is simple: they are operating under the misguided notion that in order for the church to keep its vitality, you need to leave it alone ("If it ain't broke. . ."). In fact, the opposite is true. In order for that same vitality to remain, you need to keep changing it—keep pouring God's living water through the aqueduct instead of damming it up.

Churches deteriorate when they have not refreshed their spirits, just as fences grow gray and cracked if they are not repainted.

:: THE ART OF TELLING FISH STORIES ::

So, I will boast all the more gladly of my weaknesses, so that the power of Christ may dwell in me. —*2 Corinthians 12:9*

People who listen to my preaching always manage to help me keep humble. I've found that no matter what subject I use as an illustration, someone in the audience knows a different perspective or has more complete information, and they'll usually tell me about it. For instance, I once made this comment during an evangelism sermon: "You can't expect fish to just jump into your boat. You have to go fishing for them." Sure enough, one of the men of the church came up to me later and told me the story of the time he was out fishing and a fish jumped right into the boat! Well, I stand corrected! On more than one occasion I have been nailed for mixing metaphors, mismatching information (like the time I called the Lone Ranger's horse "Trigger"), or mangling mathematics. Well, at least they were listening!

We are so very exposed when we are standing in front of people wagging our tongues, so very vulnerable to being seen for what we are: fallible human beings. I've found that it helps to have a good sense of humor about myself—to laugh at my mistakes, and to be receptive to the corrections. It's not always easy.

A seminary professor drilled into my class that we should preach *what we know.* When he said that, he wasn't talking about fishing or mathematics. He was telling us not to worry about the passages of Scripture that we don't understand. There are enough that we do understand to last a lifetime of preaching. Still, there is something about that comment that connects with my heart as well as my brain. John Calvin once made the observation that knowing God and knowing ourselves are twin concepts. We can't know God without knowing ourselves, and vice versa. So, when we preach about God, we need to reveal some things about ourselves, too. God speaks not around us but through us. That means that our life journey has a place in our preaching. When we share something of our own struggle and success in faith, we help people to connect with God themselves.

I don't mean we should give a point-by-point travelogue of our last fishing trip (boring). Or the gory details of Aunt Matilda's gall bladder operation (X-rated). Or tell what our spouse said in disgust as we went out the door in a huff (unfair). But when we share the gospel, we must share our selves as well. Isn't that what God did for us?

:: FISH UNTIL DARK ::

Even though I walk through the darkest valley,
I fear no evil; for you are with me; your rod and your staff—
they comfort me. —Psalm 23:4

A well-known fact about fishing is that no matter what the fishing has been like all day, it will improve just as darkness settles on the river. Like many of us, fish like a little bedtime snack. I have seen some pretty nice fish brought in right at dusk. So, as the shadows lengthen and the orange glow turns slate gray, the die-hard anglers will take off their polarized sunglasses and dig in their vests for their night lights. And they will keep fishing, even though they no longer can be sure if the ripple in the water is a rise or just a skiff of wind. Me? I just make sure I am not far from shore. Night is no time to be stuck in the middle of a hole too deep to wade.

Deep water is only one hazard at dusk. One night I was determined to fish all the way to the darkness, when all of a sudden a flock of brownish birds swooped by—a little close for comfort, I might add. A closer look revealed that they weren't birds at all, but bats! They, too, like a little night fishing—though they are not after the fish, but the same bugs the fish are after. I have proof. On another evening, I saw numerous fish rising on the bank opposite from where I was standing. The river was just wide and deep enough to keep me from quite reaching them. Then I saw a couple of rises more toward the middle. I went for the closer fish with my rusty spinner. Apparently, the spinner looked pretty authentic, because when it lit on the surface of the water, a hungry bat swooped down and grabbed it (and the metaphor "blind as a bat" bites the dust). I was pleased that my fly was so realistic, but it created a new dilemma: What was I going to do with a flailing bat at the end of my line? I wanted to release it as kindly as I would a fine trout. But, well, it was a bat! I know that all those stories of blood-sucking are fairy tales, but I wasn't going to get any closer than I had to. I reeled it in a ways, and then stepped up and clipped the leader off. And I wished the bat well, hoping it wouldn't choke to death on my spinner.

In life, as in fishing, the dark does harbor hazards that are not present in the light. Still, as fishers of people, we need to discipline ourselves to fish until dark. We need to learn to be unintimidated by the dark times in people's lives and the dark night of our own soul. Not long ago, I sat in a hospital conference room with some family members who were faced with a tough decision. A relative had collapsed and become unconscious. His heart had stopped beating, and he wasn't breathing. By the time the paramedics arrived, he had been without oxygen for a considerable length of time. Still, they were able to resuscitate him and get his heart beating again. But he remained unconscious. Medically, there was no real hope of a recovery, so after a few days passed, the closest family members were faced with the decision of whether to remove the life support. It's not a decision that any of us want to make. Yet, it is a very real part of life.

For the past couple years, an older couple in our congregation has been facing an increasingly dark period. She has Alzheimer's disease and is in a nursing home; he has had to give up his driver's license because of failing eyesight. It's been a struggle for them, yet they are both an inspiration. Each time I visit Audrey, my spirits are lifted. She remembers me, if not my name, and she gives me that bright smile of hers. I remember her faith, and I smile, because I know that God has not forgotten her. When I speak to Larry, he may share some of his pain and questions, but he also shares a laugh, a light-hearted moment, a smile.

My responsibilities in the presbytery have brought me close to dark times in the lives of pastors and their congregations as well: colleagues caught in misbehavior and disciplined by the church; pastors wrongly accused and seeking vindication; congregations and pastors at odds with each other and despairing of finding the key to a new relationship, fearing the loss of members and giving and ministry.

In many and various ways, we walk through the valley of the shadow of death. It's important that we not run from the darkness or pretend that all is well. That will only delay receiving the grace of God. I have often said that God does the best work of ministry when life is at its worst. Why? Because it is at those times that we are most aware of our need. The emptiness is undeniable. People reach for spiritual and emotional support at times of great loss and struggle. When all is well, when life is at its fullest and success is at every turn, people tend to get a false sense of security; a sense that the material world is all there is and human strength is adequate to sustain life. When physical life is ebbing away, people often grasp for the more lasting spiritual realities. When a church is in trouble, there is the opportunity to challenge false gods and inspire faith. When we ourselves are in a time of darkness, there is the opportunity to receive the grace of God and to model a life of integrity and transformation.

So, fish until dark. But do it with discernment, because the fish are not the only hungry ones. It won't be bats who will try to snatch hope from those who desperately need it, but the enemy of the soul.

84 :: THE ONES THAT GOT AWAY ::

I planted, Apollos watered, but God gave the growth.
—*1 Corinthians 3:6*

I heard a rumor yesterday. It seems that a family from our church has started going to the church down the street. I immediately had two reactions, one quite logical and the other deep in my gut. The logical reaction went like this: Well, they have never really settled into this church anyway. They've never been quite happy with the informal style of worship. They've always stood just a little bit at a distance, not quite fully committed, not responsive to the challenges toward discipleship that others have responded to. They'll be better off, more than likely, at the other, more traditional, church. The other reaction was a deep sense of failure. If someone leaves us for another church, I must have done something wrong.

My brain tells me that one church can't please every fish in the sea. Nor should it. We need to be who we are and to celebrate the fact that other churches are able to minister to the people that we can't quite reach. But my heart is in another place altogether. I want them all. And I want them all to be happy with me and with *my* church.

Did you ever notice that when anglers come home from a fishing trip, they regale people with stories about the one that got away? Sometimes it almost seems that the ones that get away provide the greatest adventure, the most mystique, and the greatest challenge because they are still "out there" waiting for us to try again. But not so in the church. The ones that slip off the hook are a personal failure, a blow to the ego.

Ah, so there it is! The all-important ego. I feel bad about losing a few fish, because then my membership statistics don't look as good, the stewardship drive may not come up quite as high—but not because I care for the fish.

We will have cause to grieve if we genuinely lose the fish. The

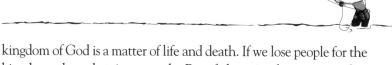
kingdom of God is a matter of life and death. If we lose people for the kingdom, then that *is* a tragedy. But if they simply go to another church, then they are not really lost, are they?

:: FOUL-HOOKED FISH ::

"I asked your disciples to cast it out,
but they could not do so." —Mark 9:18b

An important goal of catch-and-release fishing is to release the fish unharmed. Fishing with barbless hooks helps a great deal. I keep a surgical hemostat hanging on my vest, as do many fly fishers, to make hook extraction kinder and quicker. In a perfect catch, the fish comes to the surface with a fly lightly hooked in its lip. It's a simple matter, then, to quickly slip off the hook, and let the fish slide gently back into the water. It's tough, though, to safely extract a fly that the fish has swallowed. It can also happen that a fish gets entangled in weeds at the bottom of the river. (Big brown trout are notorious for diving to the bottom and holding on for dear life.) From time to time, a gymnastic trout will do some surface-water acrobatics and end up sideswiping a fly with its gills. In fishing language, we call that "foul-hooking the fish."

Very often, it's not the fish's fault. There's the relative skill and experience of the angler to take into account. I confess that I am still sometimes surprised by the quickness and slipperiness of the fish, and in their flailing about I sometimes lose my grip, so that my release is less than quick and my method less than graceful.

I remember one particular fish that I was proud to catch. I had been watching it take caddis flies near the riverbank under the overhang of a tree. It was a difficult cast, but I made it, and as it turned out, I tricked the fish into taking the fly. The fish danced for me a couple of times and then obediently started coming toward me as I reeled in. The overhanging branches got in the way though, and the fish ended up getting tangled. Carefully, though not skillfully, I managed to get it disentangled, only to find the hook deeply embedded. The kind thing would have been to cut off the fly and let the fish go, but I was determined to use my hemostat. By the time I was done, the poor fish was weary and, I fear, wounded. I held it in the water, like all the books tell you to do, to revive it. The fish flicked its tail weakly, and I let it go. Down the stream it went, belly up.

I went back to the cabin discouraged, no longer proud of my catch. I still wonder about that fish. Did it survive my awkward efforts at setting it free? Or did it die an ungracious death on the banks of that river?

In our work of ministry, it is also true that not all of the fish are released unharmed. There are people who are wounded in their experience in the church.

I know that there are so-called anglers who are genuine predators. To paraphrase a metaphor from Jesus, such a predator "does not care for the fish" (see John 10:13). Those who are predators are in the ministry for some other reason than catching people for the kingdom of God and releasing them for ministry. Maybe it's money or power, or maybe it's revenge for something deep in their past. But it's not the predators who concern me here. It's those of us who genuinely want to do ministry that is wholesome and fruitful and have no desire to foul-hook our fish. Yet, sometimes through our own mistakes or misjudgments, we do. A careless word, a selfish act, a comment made in ignorance, and there are hurt feelings and misunderstandings.

I've found that there's no escaping it, this business of being imperfect. The longer I am in the ministry, the more I am aware of my own inadequacies. I remember one young woman I knew early in my ministry whom I tried to release gently but who ended up feeling worse. And a couple that Ed and I tried to help restore their marriage—it got worse instead of better, and they blamed us. When Ed and I decided to split our efforts and work for a time in two different churches, I quickly became aware that I could not meet everyone's

expectations. There were some hurt feelings and a few misunderstandings. I found myself apologizing more than usual and having
many long conversations—and feeling guilty, worried that some people would leave because of my inadequacies.

Just as there will always be arguments in marriage, there will
always be pain in the midst of ministry. No matter how hard we try
to hone our skills and minister from the heart, we will fail from time
to time, with some people. What to do? Well, realism is a good place
to start. Don't expect to be something you are not (that is, something other than human). Count on it. You will fail. Period. But as
we preach to others, we must preach to ourselves. Failure is not the
end, but an opportunity for grace. Those who are able to admit their
humanity and who are willing to grow from experience will do so,
and will be respected by their congregations. Those who insist on
keeping the pretense of perfection will, sooner or later, be seen for
the frauds that they are. Realism that leads to repentance opens the
door for grace, not just for ourselves, but for those who have been
harmed by our bumbled attempts at ministry. Back when I was in
seminary, I had a friend who was probably one of the best parents I
have ever known. She loved her two little girls deeply. Yet, she was
also painfully aware that she couldn't be everything to them that
they needed. So, every night she would slip into their bedroom and
silently pray that God would "make up the difference" between the
love she had been able to give the girls and the love they needed.

God is not limited by our inadequacies. God can—and will—
make up the difference between the love we have been able to give
and the love that our people need.

:: TRUE CONFESSIONS ::

*Proclaim the message; be persistent whether the time
is favorable or unfavorable.* —2 Timothy 4:2

88   I've often thought I'd be better at fishing if it weren't for a particular character flaw: I feel sorry for the fish. Sure, most of them are smarter than I am and there are a whole lot more that get away than end up in my net (maybe *they* should feel sorry for me). But for those unlucky few that mistake my fly for a real bug, I feel sorry, guilty even, for interrupting their dinner, nicking a fin, hooking a mouth. There's no killer instinct in me.

   I know what all the experts say. Fish don't have feelings. I remember my dad saying the same thing about the worms that I jammed onto the hook as a kid. They don't feel a thing. The uneasy feeling has never quite left me, though. Maybe they do have feelings. Is it right to toy with them that way? To tease them, hook them, reel them in and then set them loose just to be caught all over again? It might be better just to knock them over the head and be done with it instead of subjecting them to this repetitive torture.

   Feeling sorry for the fish does nothing for my casting ability or my ability to psych out my prey. My motivation sags and with it my productivity. It's an emotional/ethical dilemma that I will have to work out over time.

   My feelings for the fish remind me of a neurotic tendency that many Christian leaders have toward their people: they feel sorry for them. That sounds like it ought to be a good quality in a leader, but it's not. By "feel sorry," I don't mean compassion. We must have compassion for those whom we serve, or we cannot truly serve them. But feeling sorry for people may lead us to rob them of legitimate suffering. In other words, feeling sorry may lead to codependent leadership, leadership that gives people what they think they want instead of the grace and truth of God. This kind of leadership seeks to make people feel good instead of working with them as they experience necessary growing pains. I wish I had a nickel for every time I've heard someone say, "But I don't want to hurt this person's feelings." Helpful confrontation is avoided, and conflict festers instead of being resolved.

   It's like the person in the novel *Zorba the Greek* who felt sorry for

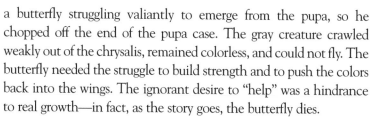

a butterfly struggling valiantly to emerge from the pupa, so he chopped off the end of the pupa case. The gray creature crawled weakly out of the chrysalis, remained colorless, and could not fly. The butterfly needed the struggle to build strength and to push the colors back into the wings. The ignorant desire to "help" was a hindrance to real growth—in fact, as the story goes, the butterfly dies.

I knew a pastor who handled conflict between members by saying, "If you've got a problem with each other, you've got to come through me." He "settled" disputes by placating each side, sometimes with conflicting statements. Both persons in the conflict felt better, but neither learned how to resolve conflict on their own. And the same conflicts continued to emerge over and over again.

Parents sometimes "rescue" their children to the point where they don't have to live with the consequences of their actions. Denominational leaders sometimes "rescue" congregations or pastors instead of walking beside them and helping them grow through legitimate suffering.

What might have been different about the message of the Old Testament prophets if they had *felt sorry* for Israel? What if Paul had *felt sorry* for the poor Christians in Corinth? Would a watered-down message communicate the word of God? Paul warned his protégé, Timothy, that the time would come when "people will not put up with sound doctrine, but having itching ears, they will accumulate for themselves teachers to suit their own desires" (2 Timothy 4:3). My friends, that day has already arrived. The question is, Do we want to preach God's gracious and challenging Word, or do we want to preach in a way that will make people like us?

As Christian leaders we need to be compassionate toward those whom we serve, but we must learn to be dispassionate as well, so that we do not absorb the other person's pain. It's a boundary issue. We can do a lot for other people, but we can't take responsibility for them. They must take charge of their own feelings, decisions, and actions. They must respond to the Word of God for themselves. We can't do it for them.

:: FISHING AS THERAPY ::

"I have said these things to you so that my joy may be in you, and that your joy may be complete." —John 15:11

My husband has a T-shirt that says, "For the rich, there's therapy, for the rest of us, fishing." Amen to that. A few days of fishing a favorite stream are worth many sessions in a therapist's office. And that is as it should be. Jesus said it himself. After his famous "vine and branches" sermon, where he talks about the importance of fruitfulness and the prerequisite of abiding in him, he concludes with this statement: "I have said these things to you so that my joy may be in you, and that your joy may be complete" (John 15:11).

Following Christ and pursuing our ministry has a therapeutic effect. Christ makes us whole while we are reaching out to others. Frederick Buechner says it so aptly when he describes a Christian's vocation as the "place where your deep gladness and the world's deep hunger meet."[5]

A Chinese proverb suggests that if you want to be happy for an hour, get drunk; if you want to be happy for a few days, get married; if you want your happiness to last all week, kill your pig and eat it; but if you want your happiness to last forever, you need to learn to fish.

Considering the analogy of the vine and branches, this makes sense. Think of all that grace flowing from Jesus through you to other people. Some of it is bound to rub off on its way through. The analogy also assumes that you are ministering to others with the strength that God supplies, not your own. You know the difference when you experience that state of being that we call "burnout." Our own strength has limits. God's doesn't. And God's strength comes in a balance with rest and renewal.

Just be careful not to twist this thought into the idea that your

---

5. Frederick Buechner, Wishful Thinking: A Theological ABC (New York: Harper and Row, 1973), 95.

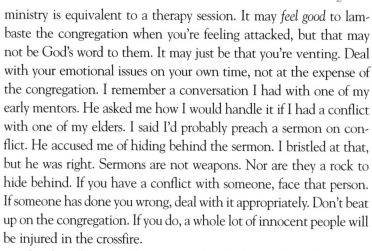

ministry is equivalent to a therapy session. It may *feel good* to lambaste the congregation when you're feeling attacked, but that may not be God's word to them. It may just be that you're venting. Deal with your emotional issues on your own time, not at the expense of the congregation. I remember a conversation I had with one of my early mentors. He asked me how I would handle it if I had a conflict with one of my elders. I said I'd probably preach a sermon on conflict. He accused me of hiding behind the sermon. I bristled at that, but he was right. Sermons are not weapons. Nor are they a rock to hide behind. If you have a conflict with someone, face that person. If someone has done you wrong, deal with it appropriately. Don't beat up on the congregation. If you do, a whole lot of innocent people will be injured in the crossfire.

Similar advice can be given to lay leaders in the church. An interesting dynamic that often crops up among church leaders is a struggle for power. I've observed that it's often those who have been disempowered in their personal life or at work who often struggle for power at church. Maybe they weren't promoted to the expected rank or position at work. Maybe they have a domineering or abusive spouse. While they claim to be seeking a place to serve, what they really want is a place to be okay. But they assume that having "power" is what makes them okay. Such power, when achieved, though, is dysfunctional at best, and often cripples the church. Genuine power comes from knowing that in God's sight we are loved and forgiven and healed. Service that flows out of *this* relationship has real power.

We don't have to mope around all the time, stressed out and burned out. If we stay connected to Christ instead of going off on our own power, our work will bring us joy, because that relationship brings us joy. Remember those stories in Acts about the disciples singing in prison? They weren't nuts. They just had a great secret. God was alive in them.

Yes, there will be tough times, and yes, there will be pain and struggle. But if there is not also some measure of joy, then it may be time to consider a new calling.

5 :: THE LAST CAST

*When [Paul] had finished speaking,
he knelt down with them and prayed.
There was much weeping among them all;
they embraced Paul and kissed him,
grieving especially because of what he had
said, that they would not see him again.*
—*Acts 20:36–38*

THE MOST DIFFICULT CAST of a fishing trip is the last one. I am usually one of the last ones to pack it in. You never know—the next cast might produce the big one. Besides, for those of us who don't live near the river, it will be a long time before we come again.

Whether or not the trip has been a good one in the fish department, I find that my attitude is the same. I don't want to leave. I want one more chance for victory, one more chance for that trophy picture and bragging rights. One more cast.

Breaking down the rods and getting the fly-tying bench ready for travel is always a bittersweet task. The memories are sweet, but saying goodbye to the river is painful. I'm not ashamed to say that sometimes I have cried, because the peace of the river has been so profound and my needs so great.

It's hard to say goodbye to the river and the fish, but it's not hard to know when to say goodbye. That has been predetermined by our reservations. Vacation is over, like it or not. In ministry, it's not so easy. When is the right time to make the last cast in a particular ministry? When is the right time to say goodbye and move on?

:: SAYING GOODBYE ::

It's always tough for me to say goodbye. Going to a new place is exciting, but leaving is excruciating. It doesn't matter whether it's been a good ministry or a painful one. Leaving is tough. So much is unfinished, so much could still be done, if only . . . if only. . . .

In my first long-term pastorate, I bonded thoroughly with my congregation. Meanwhile, I had met Ed and we had married. He went through seminary, and started looking for a call. We started talking about serving a church together. I wasn't really open to it at first, because I wasn't ready to leave my congregation. So, he looked unsuccessfully for a position within commuting distance. During that time, we went on study leave some distance away, but I returned for a speaking engagement on the weekend. Though I had pulpit supply for my congregation, I went to church that Sunday morning. As I sat in the congregation I had an uncanny feeling, one that I had not had before, nor have I had since. It was an emptiness. There's no other way I can describe the feeling. I felt as if the Holy Spirit had been removed from the relationship. Not that God no longer had plans for the congregation or for me, but that it was no longer to be "us." It was startling but undeniable, and from then on, I began the search process with Ed, and ultimately we were called to a co-pastorate.

The knowledge of God's leading did not make the leaving less painful. But it made it possible. Each move since then has been equally difficult to accept, even when it has been frighteningly clear that the time to go was imminent.

When Ed turned sixty, we began to talk in earnest about retirement. We have found it an awkward conversation, given our age difference (I am thirteen years his junior). He is not ready to quit ministry, and I am nowhere near retirement. But he is beginning to think toward some distinct changes in his life. He wants to do more fishing, for one thing. Our first tentative steps toward the unknown began with him taking a leave of absence from our shared ministry and taking on an interim position. We are not yet sure what lies beyond this transitional stage. But what has helped us to find a measure of freedom in the midst of not knowing is to trust each other—to refuse to be in denial about our differences and to talk about our fears and hopes. Even more, to trust that God—who led us to the river in the first place—will be the one to lead us back home as well.